FIGHTER FOR INDEPENDENCE

Jawaharlal Nehru

1889–May 27, 1964

India is a land of contrast and contradiction—and no one better typifies its complex character than the man who helped lead it to independence. This is the dramatic story of Jawaharlal Nehru, an aristocrat who became Prime Minister of India and the idol of the masses. An admirer of English culture, he sacrificed wealth and freedom to struggle against British rule. A fiery nationalist, he sought international understanding against fierce odds.

FIGHTER FOR INDEPENDENCE

Jawaharlal Nehru

WITHDRAWN-CMU

by

Alfred Apsler

JULIAN MESSNER   **NEW YORK**

Published by Julian Messner
Division of Pocket Books, Inc.
8 West 40 Street, New York 10018

© Copyright 1966, 1963 by Alfred Apsler

Fourth Printing, 1966

Printed in the United States of America
Library of Congress Catalog Card No. 66-17094

To my wife
Erna

CONTENTS

CONTENTS

1.

THE TIME HAS COME

FEW INHABITANTS of New Delhi, India's capital, slept on the night of August 14, 1947. Tens of thousands had deserted the narrow lanes and choked bazaars of the Old City and had wandered along tree-lined boulevards to the pompous Council of State Building. There they stood on the huge parklike grounds amidst the maze of fashionable avenues which the British rulers had laid out. New Delhi is a planned city like Washington, D.C., dotted with round plazas into which straight streets merge like the spokes of a giant wheel.

From here the English crown had meant to rule its richest and most populous colony for centuries to come. But now, only sixteen years after the construction crews had departed, the power of government was to be handed over to the Indian people. The great awakening of dormant millions in Asia and Africa, the birth of new independent nations, had begun.

It was past eleven, but the heat still lay like a thick pall over the gathering inside the circular hall. From the ornate classical columns it seemed to reflect mercilessly upon the packed rows on the main floor. Now that the monsoon season was in full swing, the rain squalls added high humidity to the intense heat. Every movement became a chore.

In the Council Building sat the men who had carried on the fight for independence for over half a century. Perspiring freely, despite their comfortable loose garments of white homespun, the delegates of the National Congress, long out-

9

lawed and bitterly fought by the British, were waiting to become free India's Constituent Assembly.

From the galleries glinted the many-colored silks and satins of women's saris, gracefully draped over heads and shoulders. The diplomatic corps had turned out to watch and listen, and the press boxes were filled with correspondents from all over the world.

The whole assemblage was charged with the kind of electric tension that precedes moments of the utmost historical importance. The tension extended into the jammed corridors and farther out onto the wide lawns.

Under a steel-blue sky the glow of torches cast weird dancing shadows on the red-and-yellow walls of what was about to become the parliament building of the new republic. The big round sandstone structure looked half palace and half Roman circus.

Masses of dark lean bodies were everywhere. Many were clad in shapeless pajamalike garments. Some wore only loincloths. Most were barefooted. They squatted on the ground or moved around restlessly, engulfing stalled bicycle-padicabs and clumsy wooden-wheeled bullock carts.

Beyond the expanse of park could be seen more arcaded stucco buildings. They too had been destined to house colonial offices for generations to come, perhaps forever. Their Greek columns and wide French windows were strangely out of place next to the maharajas' townhouses that looked like something out of *The Arabian Nights*.

This was the funeral night for the rule of both the colonial lords and the mighty maharajas.

Excited conversation filled the night air, and much worried talk, because the astrologers had pronounced a very unfavorable horoscope. According to the stars, this was not an auspicious moment for important actions, and oldsters shook their heads in disapproval. Traditional India was influenced by horoscopes cast for weddings, for battles, even for business deals. But many young men chided their elders for their lack

of confidence. "We live in different times," they said. *"We*
fought for independence. *We* did it, not the gods. Those
were our bodies that were beaten by the bamboo sticks of the
police. Those were our leaders who were thrown into jail.
We have waited long enough."

Even more heated were the arguments about the com-
munal fighting. Independence had been bought at a terrible
price: partition of India into two countries, one for the
Hindus and one for the Moslems. With heavy hearts the leaders had agreed to partition in order to avoid civil war between brothers crazed by religious fanaticism.

Now partition was a reality, but the bloodletting had
come anyhow. Minorities trapped in the two new countries
were being massacred. Millions, in fear of their lives, were
in flight. The roads were clogged with their misery. They
were hungry, sick and, what was worse, filled with deadly
hate.

"Look what they've done to our people in Pakistan,"
shouted a young Hindu. "My brother and his whole family
were burned alive in their own house. Any Moslem that
crosses my way will not live to see the next day."

"Your grief is understandable," reasoned an older man.
"But violence only breeds more violence. It destroys what
we've been building all these years. Remember what Gandhiji
taught us."

The youth fell silent as the name of Mohandas Gandhi,
the little shriveled old man with the spiritual strength of a
saint, was invoked.

Earlier the people had watched the delegates arrive and
had cheered their well-known leaders. But as time went by,
from more and more lips came the question, "Where is
Gandhiji?"

The few who knew told the others: The father of the new
India was out of town at the moment of her birth. He felt
he was more urgently needed in Calcutta where the com-
munal bloodshed was worst. As always completely disregard-

ing his personal safety, he was throwing himself bodily between fanatic mobs of Hindus and Moslems.

But, explained those better informed, there were other
reasons for Gandhi's absence. He felt his task was done. The
Indian masses had been roused from apathy by his prophetic
voice. He had taught them the method of nonviolent struggle; now the struggle was ended. India needed a new type
of leadership, and already he had ordained his successor.

"Jawaharlal [juwähurläl'] will be our prime minister," one
man told another. "He is Gandhiji's choice."

"Jawaharlal knows the soul of the peasant. He knows what
suffering is."

"Jawaharlal has sacrificed his best years for India. He
spent over nine years in prison so we can be free."

"The gods have blessed us with Jawaharlal's leadership."

Meanwhile, the object of so much popular praise sat un-
comfortably on the platform of the assembly hall. A girls'
choir was singing, but throughout the main floor there was
an unattentive hum. From above one could see knots of
white "Gandhi caps," interspersed with blue and purple turbans, wagging with the rhythm of conversation.

Polite but unenthusiastic applause accompanied the girls
as they left the stage. Gradually the whispering ceased. A
heavy silence settled over the assembly. The rows of delegates
looked like solid white bars.

Now a solitary figure moved slowly to the rostrum. Jawaharlal Nehru appeared small and thin. The prison pallor
of his handsome face blended into the whiteness of the long
frock coat that was buttoned from the neck down to the
knees. Under the white cap the high forehead was deeply
furrowed with fatigue. Only the red rose in the third buttonhole provided a tiny dash of color.

He began to speak, but his voice faltered. Obviously he
possessed none of the assurance of a glib public orator. Emotion got in the way of performance.

Another start. This time his face lighted up. The even

voice with the unmistakable British university accent filled the hushed hall:

> . . . and now the time has come when we shall redeem our pledge, not wholly or in full measure, but very substantially. At the stroke of the midnight hour, when the world sleeps, India will awake to life and freedom. . . . The future is not one of ease or resting but of incessant striving so that we might fulfill the pledges we have so often taken and the one we shall take today. The service of India means the service of the millions who suffer. It means the ending of poverty and ignorance and disease and inequality of opportunity.

Nehru moved that the first action of the Constituent Assembly should be a solemn oath of dedication to the new, yet ancient country. A respected Moslem delegate rose to second the motion, thus dramatizing the purpose of unity.

The crystal in the giant chandeliers tingled as the delegates rose in a mighty prolonged cheer. Nehru's eyes swept slowly over the shouting men, his friends and co-workers, his cellmates in prison.

The crowd fell silent again. Only the ticking of the huge clock above the platform could be heard as its two hands moved closer to each other.

The chimes began to ring out the midnight hour. Nobody stirred. Then, out of the deep stillness rose a long wailing sound like the cry of a wounded animal. A shudder went through the bones of many who had never heard it. The sacred conch shell was being blown as it had been for more than three thousand years, in temples and on hilltops, to summon the gods as witnesses to important events.

As the sound lost itself in the farthest recesses of the hall, flashbulbs began to pop. Dr. Rajendra Prasad, an old freedom fighter and now the venerable president of the Constituent Assembly, stood at the rostrum and slowly, sentence by sentence, intoned the oath. With right arm raised everybody on the floor repeated it after him, first in Hindi, then in English:

> At this solemn moment, when the people of India through suffering and sacrifice, have secured freedom, I, a member of the Constituent Assembly of India, do dedicate myself in all humility to the service of India and her people to the end that this ancient land attain her rightful place in the world and make her full and willing contribution to the promotion of world peace and the welfare of mankind.

The first day of independence had begun, a day crowded with celebrations and official functions.

The assemblymen were still congratulating each other on the floor when Nehru and Prasad made their way to the next engagement, the official transfer of power from the foreign masters to their colony.

In the long struggle for independence Great Britain had been the enemy. But now, when victory had come, there were no hard feelings. Englishmen moved freely about the country; not a single one came to any harm. Voluntarily the spokesmen of the new country had agreed to keep it as a new dominion within the confines of the Commonwealth of Nations.

It was only half a mile from the parliament building to the palace of the last British viceroy, but the wide avenue was solidly packed with noisy crowds. Children waved small flags with the Indian colors: saffron, white and dark green with the blue wheel of Emperor Asoka in the white middle bar. Shrill outcries of joy greeted the fireworks which lighted up the slowly paling sky.

The black limousine with Dr. Prasad and Nehru could barely move, and several times it had to stop completely. Flower petals showered upon its roof.

"Jawaharlal—*Punditji*," screamed those close to the vehicle while farther away the rhythmic shout, *"Jai Hind"* ("Long live India"), filled the air.

There could be no doubt that the prime minister-to-be was the idol of the masses, and he thoroughly enjoyed his role. Gone were the signs of strain and fatigue. His blue eyes flashed merrily. Alternately he shook outstretched hands and gave the traditional greeting of *namaste* with palms together and raised to his eyes.

Finally the car came to a halt at the palace gate. Gurkha guards, rigid as statues, in high polished black boots, gold sash and blue turbans, presented arms. A young immaculately uniformed British officer, drawn saber in hand, escorted the two visitors inside.

The throne room was aglow with hundreds of lights. The future president and prime minister advanced between two rows of British officials and their Indian subordinates. Formal evening attire intermingled with uniforms of every cut and color.

From two gilded chairs under a velvet canopy rose a startlingly handsome couple, Lord and Lady Mountbatten. In his naval uniform with the many decorations and the broad red sash of his high office, the last of the once all-powerful viceroys was the embodiment of aristocratic elegance. By his side, queenly and charming, stood Lady Mountbatten in her long white satin gown, her dark hair encircled by a golden coronet.

The viceroy stepped quickly from the dais and warmly pumped Nehru's hand. Quite obviously there was a strong bond of friendship between the Britisher and the Indian. Then Lord Mountbatten returned to the dais to assume again the stiff position required by court ceremonial.

"We have come, Your Excellency," Nehru solemnly intoned, "to acquaint you with two momentous decisions. First, the Constituent Assembly has just assumed sole governing power over India as an independent and voluntary member of the Commonwealth; and secondly," his solemnity gave way to a warm smile, "in recognition of your proven love and understanding of the Indian people, the Constituent

Assembly has unanimously endorsed the recommendation
that Your Excellency serve as India's first governor general."

The governor general is the personal representative of the
British crown in a dominion. In normal times his is mostly
a ceremonial position, yet a competent and well-liked figure
can exert considerable influence.

In a simple sentence Nehru had just torn the brightest
jewel from the imperial crown. But at the same time the new
nation proffered the hand of friendship to the empire's high-
est-placed representative.

"His Majesty welcomes a free India as an equal among
equals into the bond of the Commonwealth. As for myself,"
the tall soldier-statesman spoke warmly, "I feel singularly
honored by your trust. I will try to help with the gigantic
task facing you, but I intend to retire next spring. After
that you should fill this high office with one of your own
people. In the meantime, please regard me as one of yourselves."

The official ceremony was over. There was general hand-
shaking. Those who only recently had been fighting on opposite sides of a violent struggle now inquired into the state
of each other's health and the whereabouts of their families.

Arm in arm governor general and prime minister wandered into an adjoining hall where refreshments were being
served.

"Oh, I almost forgot." Nehru reached into his coat for an
envelope and handed it to Lord Mountbatten. "Here is a
list of the cabinet members you are to swear in at noon."
Later, when the governor general opened the envelope he
found it to be empty. In the general confusion of the big
moment Nehru had forgotten to insert the list.

Despite a sleepless night the prime minister was glowing
with exuberant activity. Later in the day there would be a
big parade and the official flag-raising in War Memorial
Square. Then back to Government House where Lord
Mountbatten would take the oath of office and then in turn

swear in the Indian cabinet. Then there would be a religious ceremony performed by Hindu priests and finally a giant state dinner given by the governor general and his lady.

Jawaharlal Nehru, at fifty-eight, had become the chief executive of the second largest country in the world. This slightly built, fair-complexioned man with the contagious smile, harbored in his personality the most baffling contrasts. British jailers had robbed him of the best years of his life; yet his speech and thought were those of a British gentleman; with Mountbatten he felt a kinship of taste and outlook; in many ways he was more English than Indian.

A descendant of the most exalted branch within the priest caste, he proclaimed himself loudly an agnostic. Born to great wealth, he had espoused an ethical brand of socialism. For the cause of Indian nationalism he had sacrificed wealth and freedom of personal movement; yet he firmly believed in international cooperation. Raised in aristocratic remoteness and given to intellectual pursuits, he had become the idol of the masses. No other leader could establish rapport with the Indian peasant as he could.

Nehru was riding into the early morning light of New Delhi to meet a challenge greater than most historical figures ever had to face. Beyond the immediate danger of wholesale mob violence loomed the general plight of India: a hungry, illiterate peasantry, the confusion of many languages, pressure from impatient radicals on one side and from ultra-conservative Brahmins on the other.

He was leaving behind three decades of opposition to foreign rule, of contemplation and study in forced seclusion. Ahead was the unknown, the test of statesmanship.

2.

SACRED CORD

JAWAHARLAL NEHRU was born in the autumn of 1889. He spent his childhood years in a palatial home with extensive gardens, two swimming pools, horse stables and the first automobile imported to India.

Whoever knew the Nehru family in those days might well have predicted that this well-shaped baby would grow up to lead the typical life of India's small wealthy set. He would probably be trained in the British law and practice before courts functioning after the British model. This professional activity would leave him ample time for leisure, which he would spend in exclusive clubs with other men of his class. He would join them also in such pastimes as polo and hunting. Lengthy vacations would be spent on the French Riviera or at other international playgrounds open to those who could afford them. Of the overwhelming majority of India's humble millions he would know nothing.

Jawahar, as his family called him, was a strikingly handsome boy unashamedly spoiled by his adoring mother and by most other members of the numerous household. There was every indication that his life span would be pleasant and insignificant.

Then history threw down a challenge, and Nehru proved to be man enough to rise up to it. Like the great Buddha many centuries before him, he left the sweetly scented palace gardens and stepped into a cruel outer world to give service to his fellow men. The playboy died; the leader was born.

If we could trace the Nehru family tree back far enough we would eventually meet a light-skinned, but tough and wiry man whose name has been lost during the last four thousand years. As the west-bound American pioneers were to do ages later, he marched for many wearying months across fog-shrouded mountain passes in search of a new home. From the Himalaya he descended, footsore and parched by dust and storm, into the northern Indian plains. Behind him staggered his family, the baby riding securely on his mother's hip. They drove a flock of skinny sheep and goats before them.

This nameless ancestor belonged to one of the Aryan tribes who had left their homes somewhere in what is today central Russia. Attracted by tales of mighty rivers abundant with fish and of plains bearing lush rice fields, they had struggled across the world's most formidable mountain barrier to settle in the triangular peninsula to the south.

Under the impact of the Aryan invasion the Hindu religion developed in India. Hinduism is more than a form of worship. It is a way of thought and also a social order. It teaches that men are divided into many castes. On the top rung of the caste ladder are the Brahmins, all of Aryan origin.

Nehru's forebears were Brahmins. They settled in Kashmir, which many call the most beautiful part of India. Whoever can spare the time and money escapes the paralyzing summer heat of the cities and travels to the enchanted vale of Kashmir. There crisp cool air eternally descends from the glaciers of the Outer Himalaya range. The melting snows carried by the Jhelum River water the forests and the gardens through which wafts the scent of roses and jasmine.

Though the Nehru clan later moved to other parts of India, they proudly continued to call themselves Kashmiri Brahmins. This established them in a special elite group, high even within the exalted priest caste.

Being Brahmins Nehru's ancestors served at the temples

of Shiva, of Kali and of all the other innumerable deities. They were also scholars versed in the scriptures that had been written down in the Sanskrit language.

Sons received from their fathers the sacred white cord, the mark of their caste, and wore it around their shoulders, next to the bare skin. They had to keep themselves ritually clean and could eat only specially prepared foods. No lower-caste Hindu could share their meal or marry into their family. Contact with Untouchables was avoided like the plague. Those unfortunates, ranking even below the lowest castes, had to follow the most degrading occupations, such as sweeping the streets and removing the refuse from the homes of higher-caste Hindus. When so much as the shadow of an Untouchable fell upon a Brahmin, he considered himself defiled. Brahmins who traveled abroad contaminated themselves by eating ritually unclean food and mingling with people outside the caste system. They had to undergo complicated purification ceremonies before other members of their caste would allow them again to come near.

Early in the eighteenth century, Jawaharlal's great-great-grandfather, Raj Kaul, took his family from the cool vale of Kashmir to the sultry plain of Delhi and entered the service of the Mogul Sultan Farrukhsiar.

The Moguls had crashed out of Afghanistan's bare hills like a thunderstorm and conquered a huge empire. In between military campaigns these Moslem emperors held court in the dazzling style of the French Bourbons who ruled at the same period.

But the Moguls far outdid their European contemporaries in grandeur and refinement. To their palaces scholars and artists journeyed from as far away as Persia, Turkey and even southern Europe. The residences and tombs they erected are among the most magnificent sights of the world: domed and turreted fairy castles in glazed tile interlaced with stone tracery of unbelievable delicacy. They squandered the country's wealth, but left it covered with costly structures, such as the Taj Mahal, a peerless building of almost supernatural grace.

Family strife and overindulgence eventually reduced the Mogul sultans from powerful chieftains to mere puppets. Out of the mountainous north, raiding armies swarmed unchecked into the plains. Even Delhi, the capital city, was brutally sacked. Nobles and ambitious governors tore out pieces of the empire and ruled them independently, giving only lip service to the sultans.

To this still highly cultured, but now powerless, shadow court came Raj Kaul. The Moslem ruler warmly welcomed the Brahmin who had a reputation as a student of Sanskrit and Persian literature. The common bond of artistic and intellectual interest was stronger than the dividing bars of religion or nationality.

Instead of paying Raj Kaul a salary, the sultan followed the custom of the time and granted the court scholar an estate with a mansion on it. The house stood on the bank of a canal. The Urdu word for canal is *nahar*. Raj Kaul added the word "nehru" (the person who lives by the canal) to his name, but as time went on the other words were dropped, and only Nehru remained.

The first Nehru's sons and grandsons became legal advisers to the Mogul court. In long robes, according to Persian style, with ornamental curved swords at their sides, they went about their duties amidst the marble screens, the heated pools and the preening peacocks of the royal gardens.

In the meantime, European colonizers were swarming inland from their coastal strongholds eager to scoop up India's precious stones and rare spices. They engaged in violent contests among themselves over the privilege of exploiting the wealth of the subcontinent. Complete victory fell in time to the British East India Company, a group of cunning Englishmen who had banded together for the profitable marketing of Indian exotic goods.

The exploits of the East India Company form one of the

most amazing chapters in world history. Under a charter granted by the British king, a few merchants had set out in flimsy vessels to do some trading in indigo, muslin and gold-embroidered silks. They ended up ruling an empire many times the size of the motherland.

Adventurers who had come to amass quick fortunes found themselves, against all intentions, in the roles of diplomats, judges and generals. They intervened in the endless disputes between petty native princes. They sent Indians to prison and to the gallows. Armies of native soldiers snapped to attention at their command.

Like a giant spider, the company spun its web wider and wider across the valleys of the Indus and the Ganges, the highlands of the Deccan and the steaming tropical forests of the South, until all India was at its mercy. At long last the country was united—by enslavement from without.

In the London meeting room of the company directors, the fate of untold millions was determined. But while the financiers collected huge dividends on their investment, India suffered.

Too many peasants were trying to eke out a living from the worn-out soil of their postage-stamp–sized farms. There were no factories in the cities to absorb the surplus of labor, for the company discouraged the development of native industry. The Britishers wanted raw material but no competition for their garment factories back home. The men and women of India should raise the cotton but buy from England the clothes that had been made out of it.

Over the villages was let loose a locust swarm of tax gatherers who, after squeezing enough out of the peasantry to satisfy the company, lined their own pockets with money. More and more small farmers ended up as landless tenants at the mercy of the landlords. The native princes closed their eyes to the deteriorating state of affairs; they had been bribed into submission.

Confusion and misunderstanding grew. Finally the accumulated discontent and hate exploded in the bloody rebellion of 1857.

It began with a mutiny of native company troops. Then, in her hurt pride, India remembered the shadow emperors who were still holding court in Delhi. Patriots wanted to restore the decadent Mogul dynasty to its former glory so that the country could rally around it and drive out the foreign exploiters.

It was all in vain.

The last Mogul prince was not the man for the job. It would have taken a dedicated genius to galvanize the scattered bands of rioters into a mighty people's army. The cannon and the military skill of the company agents prevailed. The rebellion drowned in a sea of blood, and the prince fled into exile.

Blue-eyed, red-bearded Pandit Ganga Dhar Nehru, Jawaharlal's grandfather, had served as the capital city's chief of police during the final agony of the Mogul era. The flight of the last ruler was also the end of his career. During the massacres and pillages that followed the revolt, he lost all his possessions. Even the family papers went up in flames. Ganga Dhar and his family barely escaped with their lives. With thousands of others they took to the road and marched to the city of Agra, which had once been the capital.

Only by a stroke of good luck did the Nehrus survive this trek. Had not one of Ganga Dhar's sons acquired a fair command of conversational English, they might never have arrived at Agra. His young daughter had a very light complexion. Fair skin is common in the family, but this girl must have had more than her share of the trait. The refugees ran into a band of roaming English soldiers who thought she was British and had been kidnapped. In those days it took less than that to hang a group of Indians to the nearest trees. The girl's brother frantically drew upon his whole English vocabulary to explain the situation. The soldiers might not have believed him in the end, but matters were delayed long enough for other travelers to come by and confirm his story. Only then were the Nehrus allowed to move on.

In Agra, a short distance from the Taj Mahal, Ganga Dhar died at the age of thirty-four, and Motilal, Jawaharlal's father, was born three months later. Since Motilal's oldest brother was not living at home, responsibility for the care of the family fell to the second brother, Nandhal, a lawyer. Motilal loved him with the affection of a son for his father.

Though the revolt had been crushed, the time of the British East India Company was up. Aroused public opinion demanded a change. The trading company was dissolved, and India became a colony directly ruled by the British crown. In a splendid ceremony Queen Victoria was enthroned as empress of India. Her representatives, the viceroys, assumed nearly absolute power.

The company agents were replaced by a small army of government officials. They settled in spacious bungalows that stood in walled-in gardens. Brown-skinned servants in great numbers ministered to all their wants. Even the master's dog often had its own servant.

The tightly knit ranks of British civil servants formed a new supercaste, imposed above the old caste system. Their fancy clubs were closed to all who called India their home unless they were the white man's servants. The daily problems of those below their exalted status, the hopes and fears of the real India, bothered them not at all. They closed their eyes and ears, preferring to know nothing.

In the cities, there were now small groups of Indians whose livelihood depended on the British rule and who found this very profitable. They held the lower positions in the civil service hierarchy, or they appeared as attorneys at court. The wealthy engaged in business deals with England and grew wealthier.

These Indians lived in a strangely conflicting world. They wanted to impress the British with their own cultural heritage. Their homes resembled miniature Mogul courts. But they were also anxious to ape the West in dress and manner. Their children were sent to British schools. Never completely accepted by their European acquaintances as social equals, they prided themselves on wining and dining them in their luxurious homes. The Nehrus belonged to this tiny segment of India's population.

Nandhal moved the family to Allahabad (al'uhubad') in the plains of northern India to practice before the High Court which the British had established. Allahabad is only surpassed by Benares as a shrine of Hinduism. Located on the confluence of the sacred river Ganges and two tributaries, it overflows with pilgrims, especially during the numerous religious festivals.

There, under the loving care of his brother, Motilal grew up to become a strong-willed, commanding personality. He studied first only Persian and Arabic and was admired for his wide knowledge in those fields. In his teens he turned to English. From then on he dressed like a European and was generally attracted by Western ways at a time when this still caused lots of raised eyebrows.

He delighted in shocking old-fashioned fellow Brahmins with his contempt of time-honored practices. After returning from a trip abroad, he upset the peace of the whole Allahabad community and caused a great controversy when he refused to undergo the tedious purification rites that were prescribed after such "defilement."

As an adolescent, Motilal was the acknowledged leader of a noisy crowd that got into all kinds of scrapes. He loved fights of any description. Wrestling was one of his favorite sports. From the gymnasium he carried this delight in contests into the courtroom, where he became an outstanding master of the legal argument.

Motilal married twice. Each time the marriage was arranged by the family, as was the Indian custom. Shortly after the birth of a son he lost both his first wife and the child. Then his relatives found him a dainty doll-like Kashmiri girl. Swaruprani was her name, but friends and members of the family called her Rani. She was thirteen years old when they were married. Jawaharlal was her first child and only son.

The older Nehru never finished his university studies, but passed the bar examinations with highest honors. From then on his apparently inexhaustible energy was divided between accumulating considerable wealth and spending it lavishly on comfort and amusements. He lived life to the fullest. His loud, sustained laugh was famous all over the city.

Europeans, Moslems, Hindus and Sikhs—all enjoyed Motilal's luxurious hospitality. Almost every night a lively circle met at his home. There they toasted each other's health with strong spirits no pious Brahmin would ever touch. They ate, played and talked in a climate of well-heeled Western sophistication.

This was the world in which Jawaharlal Nehru spent his boyhood.

3.

LONELY SPLENDOR

LAUGHTER AND GAY CONFUSION reigned in the sun-drenched streets of Allahabad. It was the feast of Holi, and everybody seemed determined to make the most of it. For the poor—and that included the vast majority—it was a rare interruption of their monotonous lives. They shouted and sang to the din of drums and cymbals. Snake charmers and vendors of sweets squatted in the dust. Swarms of children roved the streets, joyously squirting everybody with colored water. That was their privilege of the day.

Jawahar was scared. The little boy nervously clutched a water pistol that was filled wth a horrible purplish liquid. His thin lips were tightly pressed together. They had sent him from his nearby home and ordered him to have fun.

A band of boys approached. They were dressed in ragged clothes, formerly white but now spotted like much-used painter's palettes. Jawahar knew some of them by sight—the sons of family servants.

"Look, Motilal's son," shouted a tall coffee-brown boy. "What a fancy outfit. Come, let's give it a good washing."

They surrounded him and let go with their squirt guns. In a matter of seconds Jawahar's blue sailor's suit was covered with yellow, brown and pink blotches. The wet fabric clung to his shivering skin.

He managed a weak artificial smile and jerked at his own weapon. Quickly the tormentors retreated to a safe distance.

27

The purplish water dropped to the ground and formed a little dark puddle in the street dust.

"Coming with us, fellow?" asked a short fat youngster.

For a moment Jawahar's face lighted up. He advanced a few steps, then hesitated.

"Aw, we're not good enough for the lawyer's son," sneered the big brown boy. "Even on Holi he must act like the British." He strutted a few steps, holding himself ramrod stiff, his nose up, in what was supposed to be an imitation of an Englishman. The others roared with delight, and went off, leaving Jawahar by himself.

With a soggy sleeve he tried to wipe his face, streaked with dust, greenish water and a few tears. For a while he stood staring after the boys. Then he turned and ran toward home.

Home for Jawahar was the largest and most luxurious house in Allahabad. His father had purchased it only recently to indicate his success and growing wealth. He had named it Anand Bhawan (Abode of Happiness). With its colonnades and awning-shaded balconies, the three-storied building would have made a perfect mansion for any substantial country squire in rural England. Spacious lawns surrounded the main structure, and a little farther off were tennis courts and orchards.

Amidst all this splendor, in a house full of people, Jawahar —the name means "red jewel"—was a lonely child with no playmates of his own age. His two sisters were too young. One was born when he was eleven, and the other not until he had left to study in England, at the age of fifteen.

More then twenty relatives lived in Anand Bhawan. This is not unusual where the traditional "joint family" system prevails. The household included various cousins, but they were much older and did not want Jawahar around when they were busy with their sports and their grown-up talk.

He had no schoolmates, since his father's wealth deprived him of the experience of attending school. Instead, a succession of English governesses supervised his early education.

If one of them was young and pretty, some dashing officer stationed in the neighborhood would soon propose to her, and the Nehrus had to advertise for another governess.

Only on occasional feast days was there a chance to play with children of his own age. Birthdays and marriages offered such all-too-rare opportunities.

Of all the family celebrations, his own birthdays stand out in Nehru's memory. For once, not the father, but the boy himself was the center of attention. "I felt the hero of the occasion," he writes. "My chief grievance was that my birthday came so rarely. Indeed, I started an agitation for more frequent birthdays."

One standing custom on this day was the weighing-in ceremony. On a huge scale the boy's weight was balanced against bags full of wheat and other foodstuff which were then distributed among the poor. It was good for the poor of Allahabad that Jawahar grew heavier with every passing year.

Swarms of relatives with their numerous offspring also descended upon the Nehrus on religious holidays, which attracted immense crowds to this holy city. Then processions with dignitaries riding on white stallions and on elephants caparisoned in cloth of gold moved slowly through the streets. At such times Anand Bhawan was filled to the bursting point, and people camped on its spacious lawns. For a short time Jawahar made merry with distant relatives and was just a boy among boys.

Of course, girls came too, but the custom did not favor the mixing of the sexes at play. As Jawahar grew into his early teens the presence of girls made him self-conscious. There was no dating nor any other social contact between the young people until the parents determined the partners for marriage. Jawahar remained shy in the presence of girls and women into his manhood years.

Of necessity his most intimate personal ties were with adults. A trusted friend and confidant was Munshi Mubarak Ali, his father's venerable head servant. Often the boy retreated to Munshi's little house in the compound, sat on a soft rug and looked up to the kindly wrinkled face with the gray goatee. Respectfully he watched the pious Moslem go through the short routine of prayer performed five times a day. Then he snuggled up to the old man and, munching sticky sweatmeats, listened for hours to his stories. Munshi seemed to know all the fables and fairy tales that delighted young and old listeners in the bazaars from Calcutta to Cairo. He also liked to tell and retell the story of the great rebellion, more than forty years ago, which brought tragedy to his own family.

It began with the mutiny of the *sepoys*, the native soldiers in the service of the East India Company. The mutineers were beaten, their leaders killed by gangs of British soldiers who roamed the countryside.

Munshi was a small boy when they came to his house. They ordered his father to show them where the money was hidden, but there was no money. In their fury the soldiers made a shambles of the house and then hanged the head of the family on a tree. Often Munshi was hungry, yet he grew up strong and lean. He worked for peasants and for shop-keepers till Jawahar's uncle took him in as a personal valet.

In Munshi's tale Jawahar discovered another aspect of the relationship between India and England. He saw that it was one-sided and based on brutal force. But the fact that Munshi was kind and forgiving, not given to hating everything British, made a deep impression on the boy.

Munshi Mubarak Ali seemed to be the only male among Jawahar's closer friends who took his religion, Islam, seriously. As for the religious heritage of his family, Hinduism, it was imparted to him mainly by two women, his mother and his aunt.

Rani Nehru, Jawaharlal's mother, also a descendant of Kashmiri Brahmins, was only two generations removed from her ancestral home. Her life was completely wrapped up in the devotion to husband and children. While keeping to the

orthodox ways herself, she never objected to Motilal's mod-
ernistic transgressions. In every situation she remained the
submissive Hindu housewife. He neglected most observances
of their creed, and so the household was practically divided
into a masculine European and a little female Hindu segment.

His mother and an aunt took Jawahar along when they
brought garlands of flowers and other gifts to the various
temples and when they visited *sanyasis,* religious ascetics
who squatted motionless and almost naked in the temple
courts. From time to time they went to bathe in the Ganges.
In the ladies those acts evoked great awe and reverence, but
Jawahar just splashed cheerfully in the muddy waters without any show of devotion. Imitating the casual attitude he
saw other male members of the family take toward such
matters, he came to think that religion was something outdated and mainly a women's affair.

Rani was a tiny, slender woman with unbelievably small
hands. She had no other son, and for many years no other
child. All her affection was poured out on the handsome boy,
whom she liked to see dressed in embroidered coats of yellow
silk with matching pantaloons and jeweled slippers.

Jawaharlal confessed later that, at times, he abused his
mother's overwhelming love. It gave him a certain satisfaction to show his power over her and to wring from her
approval of all his whims. In moments of youthful sadness
the frail woman was for him a refuge. He retreated to her
friendly room when he needed solace from his loneliness and
from his father's harshness. Rani, too, knew what loneliness
was. Her health was poor, and often she had to withdraw
from the noisy social doings at Anand Bhawan.

To his mother Jawahar could confide his innermost feelings. Not so to his father. Motilal was a tower of strength, a
patriarch of whom the son later wrote that he looked and
acted somewhat like an ancient Roman senator or a Renais-
sance prince. Jawahar stood before him trembling with fear,

yet filled with limitless admiration. To grow up and be like
father was the loftiest goal that could take shape in his mind.

Motilal was given to terrible fits of temper. When his face
clouded in sudden anger, everybody, family and servants,
tried to keep as much distance between themselves and the
master as possible. Jawahar was not always successful. He
remembers one occasion when, strolling through his father's
study, he saw two fountain pens lying on the desk. Attracted
by these still rather rare contraptions and with the typical
reasoning of a six-year-old, he figured that nobody could possibly use two fountain pens at the same time. So he helped
himself to one. The result was a volcanic outburst of Father's
rage and a painful spanking. The punishment was too severe
and out of all proportion to the offense and to the age of
the offender. His mother played the Good Samaritan and
comforted her son's wounded pride.

But far from harboring any ill will, Jawahar continued to
worship the man whose charm was so irresistible.

In one field, however, the son could best his father, and
to do so gave him tremendous satisfaction. Every day he
spent hours in the outdoor swimming pool. Taught by one
of his governesses, he had become an excellent swimmer. On
sultry evenings, when relatives and friends gathered at the
pool's edge, he loved to show off his skill. Like a slender
bronzed fish he darted back and forth. He taunted those
who were afraid to venture into the deep and splashed them
till they squealed. Motilal never learned to swim properly.
Inelegantly thrashing about with arms and legs he could
barely manage to cross the pool while his son glided effort-
lessly past him and under him. Those were the most pleasur-
able moments of many a day.

The whirl of activities in which Motilal engaged left him
little time for companionship with his son. His authoritarian
airs, moreover, prevented too much familiarity. The more
precious were the rare moments when he would openly demonstrate his affection.

There were always horses at Anand Bhawan, and Jawahar became very fond of riding. Every afternoon he took his Arab pony into the country accompanied by a *sawar*, a soldier of the cavalry unit stationed in the city.

One afternoon, as they were passing through a ramshackle village, the road was blocked by a commotion. There had been an accident involving one of the innumerable sacred cows that roam the country. The very air was charged with dynamite. Loud shrieks rose from the crowd. The nervous Arab reared. What a queer feeling, thought Jawahar as he went sailing through the air.

Then he found himself sitting on the ground, the *sawar* bending over him in mortal fright. It was he who would have to answer if any harm befell the boy. But Jawahar was unhurt, only a little shaken up and quite dirty. The soldier helped him up. They looked for the pony. It was gone.

Uneasily Jawahar mounted behind the *sawar*, and they began the sad homeward trip on the sturdy cavalry horse. He was thinking of his father's temper.

As they turned a corner he saw him. Motilal was driving the car, the only one in the city. He stopped and rushed out. The wonder vehicle was immediately surrounded by a curious crowd. House guests in tennis dress and servants appeared from the side streets where they had begun a hastily organized dragnet search.

Motilal pulled his son from the horse and hugged him, half-laughing, half-crying. "Thank heaven you're all right." He tapped the youngster's back and shoulders as if to see whether he was still all in one piece. "We were so frightened when the pony appeared by the tennis courts without you. Through my mind ran dreadful visions. I—I—"

He stammered. Jawahar had never seen his father speech-less. The famous courtroom orator with the silver tongue was now overwhelmed with emotion, and all because he had feared for his son's life. The big man's love could be as tempestuous as his anger.

Jawahar never forgot this incident, but Motilal showed no sign of remembering it on the same evening when, as usual, a group of military and civil officials, fellow lawyers and scholars sat around his large dining table. Anybody was welcome at dinnertime, and almost every night many showed up to sample the excellent fare and to engage in witty conversation.

A little army of immaculately liveried servants brought food from separate Eastern- and Western-style kitchens. Guests could help themselves to roast beef with Yorkshire pudding or spiced lamb curry and chutney with chopped herbs and cucumber. Bowls heaped with fragrant mangoes, papayas and other fruit were always on hand. For religious reasons a few elderly Hindus were served special vegetarian dishes.

As a little boy Jawahar used to watch such meals from behind the curtains that separated the dining hall from the kitchens. Often he saw the guests rise and perform the ritual of toasting the king-emperor. Once, when this was done with red claret, he ran terror-stricken to mother crying that Dad was drinking blood.

On another night Motilal discovered him in his hiding place and pulled him forward. Bursting into one of his ear-splitting laughs, he propped the boy on one knee and introduced him proudly, "Here you see a future barrister of great prominence. Just give him another twenty years and a good university education, and he'll outplead us all, won't you, Jawahar?" With a playful slap on the lower end of his back he dismissed the embarrassed youngster, and the conversation turned to weightier matters.

Later Jawahar was allowed to sit at the table with the grownups and listen to their talk, which could be loud and boisterous but often centered around the great ideas of mankind. The discussion drew freely upon Hindu, Moslem and Western thought. Nobody stooped to bigoted slogan-shouting, though various points of view were expounded and criticized.

Frequently the conversation turned to politics, but Motilal and his friends were interested in broad issues rather than in petty squabbles. The host himself looked down upon practical politicians as men who usually had been failures in other, more worthwhile fields. He knew that conditions were not ideal, and he was all in favor of reforms. But, like most educated and well-to-do Indians, he had no thought of separation from the Empire. Rather he wanted to say to his English friends, "We are just as good Britishers as you, and we want you to treat us as equals provided we behave as you do."

Young Nehru's education had been carefully planned by his father. It was to equal the best European civilization had to offer. When the boy had outgrown the governesses, a succession of tutors were hired who began preparing him for entrance into Harrow, the high-prestige boarding school in England that counts Winston Churchill among its alumni. Then would come Cambridge, and then the bar or the bench. Motilal could hardly foresee that his tractable, obedient son would one day not only discard these neatly laid-out plans, but even completely overturn the life pattern of his domineering father.

Among the tutors Ferdinand T. Brooks, a serious-minded, bookish young man of Irish-French parentage, exerted a strong influence upon his pupil. Brooks greatly encouraged Jawahar's lifelong habit of massive reading and saw to it that a wide range of topics were covered. Jawahar devoured everything: adventures, travelogues, biography, poetry. Among his favorites were Dickens, Scott, Thackeray, Kipling and Mark Twain. Books became substitutes for human companionship in his lonely childhood.

He also liked to read about current happenings. With great excitement he followed the Boer War (1899–1902) and the Russo-Japanese War (1904–5). His sympathies were always with the non-European underdog, the Boers, whom he considered Africans, and little Japan, the Asian David challenging the Russian Goliath.

Brooks opened for him the gates to the world of science. A little laboratory was rigged up in a spare room, and there the miracles of physics and chemistry unfolded before his entranced eyes. For quite a few years he longed to become a scientist.

All in all, it was an unusual education for a young Brahmin in a provincial Indian city.

The student also owed his tutor a significant spiritual experience. Brooks was a disciple of theosophy. The local theosophical chapter met regularly in his room with the thirteen-year-old Jawahar in frequent attendance.

Theosophy was a religious and philosophical movement founded in 1875 by a Russian. It borrowed heavily from ancient Hindu thought as expressed in the Vedas, but combined it with mystical speculations on astral bodies and occultism. The discussions were mostly beyond Jawahar's comprehension, but he was, nevertheless, fascinated. The talk of astral bodies somehow evoked in him fantasies and dreams about flying over vast distances.

Taking himself very seriously he entered Motilal's study one day.

"Father, may I have your permission to join the Theosophical Society?"

An explosion of laughter rocked the objects on the desk. "What nonsense has that crazy Irishman put into your little head now?"

"I have studied it carefully, Father, and I am very serious about it. May I?"

"All right, all right. Join to your heart's content, as long as you don't try to convert me."

The father's usual lack of reverence for spiritual matters annoyed the fledgling theosophist no end. He did join, however, and was solemnly initiated. Yet after Mr. Brooks left, he lost interest and dropped out.

Since then Nehru never felt much kinship with organized religion, especially as it had to do with ritual and ceremonies. But the theosophical episode aroused in him a lasting concern with the meaning of life. Dabbling in theosophy also deepened his interest in Hindu scripture, not as a handbook for ritual observance, but as a font of age-old wisdom.

He did not fail to notice how his nation's ancient writings gave inspiration to Europeans who had founded the movement and made up a good part of its membership. West could learn from East; it did not always have to be the other way around.

4.

FAGS AND DONS

━━━━━━━━━━━━━━━━━━━━━━━━━━━━━━━━━━

IT WAS CLOUDY AND GRAY, a real English country morning. From the eaves of the mossy stone buildings dripped the rain. The heavy gates and tiny barred windows reminded of prison, but this was Harrow, the famous training school of Britain's ruling class.

While the taxi driver unloaded several expensive-looking trunks, the Nehru family proceeded through the main gate to the headmaster's office, a bleak room, smelling of old leather, furnished with hard, uncomfortable chairs and an ink-stained rolltop desk. The headmaster himself, the Reverend Joseph Wood, D.D., received them with the air of stuffy dignity that befitted his position.

Mother Nehru and little Swarup were crying unashamedly, which earned them disapproving looks from the Rev. Wood. Motilal, however, behaved more to his liking as he gave his son some last-minute advice, trying hard, but without much success, to sound casual and witty:

"All right, old boy. Won't be seeing you for a while. Do what the masters tell you, and show the other chaps that I've taught you to behave like an English gentleman."

Some mournful kisses from mother and sister that left his cheeks wet and a last bearhug from his father, and they were gone. The headmaster conducted the pale, bone-tired boy to the "house," the dormitory where he was to stay.

He had been gone from home for some weeks, and it had been a wonderful trip with luxury liners and suites at the

Ritz and the Grand Hotel. Yesterday they had watched the horse races at Epsom Downs. But only now was he overcome by the chilling realization that he was in a strange land among strange people.

As he walked across the cobblestoned courtyard, keeping a few steps behind his fear-inspiring guide, he saw a number of his schoolmates-to-be milling about in their regulation suits with winged collars and broad-brimmed straw hats. It took him only seconds to convince himself that their stares were decidedly unfriendly. As he passed close by a little group of boys, he heard somebody snarl under his breath, "Here goes another Paramjit Singh."

Jawahar was soon to find out about Paramjit Singh. He was one of the three or four Indian boys at Harrow, all of princely families. Son of a minor maharaja, he had made himself thoroughly disliked by strutting around in fancy clothes with a gold-and-ivory walking cane, spending money right and left and always refusing haughtily to share any of his extras with the other boys. When they retaliated with some rather rough pranks, he threatened to have them trampled to death by his father's court elephants if they ever ventured near his little kingdom.

From the first day Jawahar knew that he was on probation as far as his fellow students were concerned.

Jawahar made no attempt to befriend the other Indian boys at Harrow, but did everything a good Harrowian was supposed to do. With his generous allowance he bought extra cuts of meat and sausage at the butcher's to supplement the dreary school fare, and he shared those delicacies with all his housemates.

Dutifully he submitted to the "fagging" which was the lot of lower-form boys. The young Brahmin took his turn serving as a kind of orderly and handyman for his house. He drew the baths, lighted the fires in the fireplaces and ran errands for the older boys.

Though no great hero on the playing fields, he tried his

best in the compulsory sports. On the cinder tracks he even
gained some modest honors for his, the headmaster's house,
placing third in the mile race and once winning the half-
mile event.

During the big games with Eton he sat in the stands and
raised his voice mightily when the boys broke into their
famous football song:

> Follow up! Follow up! Follow up!
> Till the field ring again and again
> With the cry of the twenty-two men.
> Follow up! Follow up! Follow up!

The daily school routine was soon familiar to Jawahar.
The school bell awakened him at seven, called him to chapel,
to classes and to the hall at mealtimes. Every day he met
with his tutor in the "pupil room" and recited his lessons
in the classics, in history and literature.

Yet despite all his good intentions, Jawahar never quite
warmed to the spirit of Harrow. He remained in the background, shy and inward-drawn.

Now that he is world-famous, biographers anxiously collect every scrap of information about his youth. They have
questioned former teachers and schoolmasters, but his impact was so modest that hardly anybody remembers him from
those days. The Reverend Edgar Stogdon, his former house-
master and assistant to the headmaster, wrote, "I would
doubt if he told many boys what his opinions were, or the
masters with whom he had a good name, as he worked well
and seldom (almost never) gave trouble."

There was a wide gap between Jawahar's interests and
those of the average Harrowian. "Most of the English boys,"
he wrote to his father, "are rather dull. They can talk about
nothing but their games."

Once he received a book as a prize for good scores in a
competitive examination. It was the first part of a three-
volume biography of Garibaldi by the famous historian

G. M. Trevelyan. Some forty years previously, Garibaldi, a most colorful and romantic character, had fought for Italian freedom. With great personal courage he had led an army of irregulars in the struggle for the unification of Italy and the expulsion of petty foreign rulers.

Jawahar became so entranced with the exploits of his new hero that he bought the other two volumes with his own pocket money. In his groping mind he drew a parallel between Italy and India: two countries so vastly different in many ways, yet similar in their fate of oppression from without and division within. He became aware of nationalism, the powerful storm that was blowing across Europe, sweeping away old regimes and artificial boundary lines. Nationalism gave peoples their first hope to govern themselves, to be masters of their own destiny.

More and more, politics became Jawahar's prime concern, overshadowing even his old love of the natural sciences. Avidly he followed political developments whenever he could get hold of newspapers and magazines.

The British general elections of 1905 had brought about a startling upset in favor of the Liberal party. A master referred to this event in class and asked the students what they knew about it. The response was completely negative, except for Jawahar. To the astonishment of the master, the recent arrival from southern Asia could name almost the whole list of the new Liberal cabinet.

Feeling confined and isolated at Harrow, Jawahar pleaded with his father, in letter after letter, to let him transfer to a university. Finally he obtained Motilal's permission. At the age of seventeen, after only two years of residence, he left the cloistered school grounds.

The boys sent him on his way with the ringing song, "Forty Years On." Clutching a dog-eared school songbook Jawahar walked through the gate with tears in his eyes. He did not regret his decision to leave, yet, at the last moment, he found he had grown quite fond of the Harrow atmosphere.

Then came Cambridge.

For three years Jawaharlal Nehru attended this great university, a place thoroughly to his liking. The stained glass in the medieval buildings, the verdant lawns of the college courts, the pathways along the sluggish river Cam so suitable for leisurely walks, the meals in the vaulted college halls: all this provided an invigorating mental climate. It invited conversation. It made it easy to pour out the thoughts that filled his mind and share them with others.

Nehru prepared for a degree in chemistry, geology and botany. But his desire to learn ranged far and wide. There was complete liberty to browse through the well-stocked libraries, to attend lectures in many fields, to meet people from all over the world, including a sprinkling of young Indians who were full of lofty ideas about their country's future. It was truly a time of intellectual growth.

Trinity College, one of the seventeen colleges that make up the university, was his temporary home. There he had his rooms, cold, but spacious and paneled in dark oak. Dignified old porters waited on him. Wrapped in the required academic gown he joined the other undergraduates at dinner. In the vaulted hall they drank their beer and talked morals and philosophy with the "dons," men of breadth and wisdom who were the tutors and university lecturers.

For the first time Nehru made friends of his own age. "We would sit by the fireside," he wrote about those days, "in the long winter evenings and talk and discuss unhurriedly deep into the night till the dying fire drove us shivering to our beds."

Still, his part in those discussions was mostly that of a listener. The man who would later improvise seven speeches a day during election campaigns could hardly bring himself to get up before a group of students and speak his mind. It was not easy to shake off the shyness of his boyhood years.

He belonged to a college debating society, the "Magpie and Stump," which had a rule that a member not speaking for a whole term had to pay a fine. The society's treasure prospered on Nehru's fines. Even in a small club of Indian students, the "Majlis," he sat silently and let the others do the arguing.

As a gentleman-scholar of means, Jawahar traveled extensively during the long vacation periods. Twice he undertook the costly voyage to India to visit his family. At other times he ranged the length and breadth of the European continent, becoming well acquainted with its museums, its castles and cathedrals.

Harrow had accustomed him to physical exercise. Wherever he went on his travels, he made use of every chance to swim, to ski and particularly to climb mountains.

His infatuation with the mountain world caused him several close brushes with disaster. On a hike across the Norwegian highlands, he decided once, more eager than wise, to take a dip in a roaring creek coming straight out of a glacier. He slipped and fell into the icy water. At once his limbs became numb and lost all sensation. He was swept rapidly along by the current. Only a few hundred yards from an enormous precipice, his English travel companion managed to get hold of his leg and drag him to safety.

From another trip he brought back an autographed picture of Count Zeppelin which is still in his possession. He received it on a visit to Berlin in 1909 when the famous builder of the first dirigible airship arrived there on a record flight. From the pioneer days of the Wright brothers to the jet era, Nehru has maintained his enthusiasm for flying.

In his studies Jawahar was moderately successful. His many interests and pleasures prevented graduation with the highest honors. But he got by comfortably and received the equivalent of a bachelor's degree.

Now came the question of a career. So much in tune was he then with the British way of life that he seriously considered a berth in the Indian Civil Service, the backbone of the colonial system. However, his inclination for any kind

of work was not very strong at that time. He was content
to drift.

So it was up to his father to make the decision for him.
Motilal decided for the law, and Jawaharlal submitted dutifully. Both father and mother were anxious to have their
only son live with them in Allahabad where he could also
practice before the High Court, whereas, as a junior member of the Indian Civil Service, he was likely to be posted
to the remotest spots of the colony.

Jawaharlal Nehru moved to London and began to prepare
himself for the bar examination. For two years he was a
member of the Inner Temple, a combination of college and
fraternity for law students. With his quick grasp of abstrac-
tions and his flair for political matters, he had a very easy
time with the study of law. Lots of hours remained to enjoy
the thrills of the big city.

London, the capital of the world's leading power, was in
the early twentieth century a splendid and proud metropolis.
The products of all continents were unloaded at her docks.
In the vaults of her banks gathered the wealth from the
four corners of the earth. For the moneyed classes it was a
time of opulent and gracious living. The mansions of elegant
hostesses were aglitter with gala parties to which the privi-
leged guests drove up in one-horse broughams. Progress and
prosperity seemed assured for a long time to come.

New ideas were also stirring. In books and from lecture
platforms critics were voicing their dissatisfaction with the
hypocrisy and the inequalities in British society. Fabian socialism sought a fairer distribution of worldly goods. Play-
wright Bernard Shaw and philosopher Bertrand Russell chal-
lenged old established concepts; and on the Continent, in
Vienna, Sigmund Freud was already expounding his revolutionary theories about the subconscious mind and the nature
of the sex drive.

Eagerly Jawaharlal plunged into the bubbling stream of
London's social and intellectual life. He sought the company

of writers, especially of poets. He also frequented the proper clubs and often turned up at the theater and at the better restaurants. Sporting a well-trimmed mustache, his shiny black hair slicked back, and dressed in the latest fashion, he became an experienced party-goer. More than once he exceeded his allowance and had to write home for more funds.

Now he found ample opportunity to keep abreast of developments in his homeland. The Indian giant was beginning to show signs of restlessness in his sleep. There were portents of change. Whiffs of crisis could be smelled in the humid air.

The Indian National Congress had been founded in 1885. Far from being the mighty rebel movement it later became, it was at first a very tame, subservient club of upper-class Hindus who politely asked for a few privileges from their British rulers. The masses of India were unaware of Congress, nor had its well-dressed members any thought of befriending the peasants or the poor of the city.

For many years Congress lived a shadowy existence, never probing below the surface of its grievances. Then the political climate began to change.

Arrogant acts on the part of the British aroused widespread indignation. Some young European-trained Hindus became impatient. Their protests took on a more vigorous note.

At school they had absorbed Western ideas of human rights and self-determination. "If those are the high principles by which Europeans want to live," they argued, "why not apply them to us? We are human too. We also want self-determination."

A new battle cry was beard among the young nationalists: "*Swaraj* [swa.räj'—self-rule] is our birthright." Not since the abortive Sepoy Rebellion of 1857 had there been such talk of massive resistance against British rule. There were bloody clashes in Bengal Province, and prisons began to fill up with revolutionaries.

Tilak, a fiery Brahmin from western India, tried to rouse Congress from its complacency. He talked of a new weapon which was to become very effective in later years—boycott. "Let us have nothing to do with British goods," he shouted, "nor with British schools. Instead of aping the enemy we must reaffirm our own Indian ways."

Congress meetings became stormy. The discussion over Tilak's fighting speeches tore its ranks asunder, and the members divided into Radicals and Moderates.

Motilal Nehru was now a prominent leader in Congress. Despite his general contempt for politicians, he had taken up politics as a side line. His whole background and personal philosophy stamped him a Moderate. The violent talk of the Radical hotheads offended his legal frame of mind and went strongly against his aristocratic, pro-British leanings.

All the while, Jawaharlal eagerly followed the news from home at his elegant quarters at the Inner Temple in London. The postman brought him large bundles of Indian newspapers and pamphlets, and he spent long hours absorbing their contents. He became an admirer of Tilak.

One day as he was reading a newspaper from Allahabad, he came upon an article written by his father. Motilal was advising caution in the demands for political changes and also had some words of praise for certain British officials whom he knew personally. This offended Jawaharlal's Radical sympathies, and in his next letter home he snapped sarcastically, "No doubt the British government is greatly pleased with your journalistic activities."

This was too much. The imperial Motilal was not used to such censure from his own children. In one of his typical outbursts of rage he threatened to cut off his ungrateful son's allowance and order him home immediately. But the storm blew over, and Jawaharlal could stay on to finish his studies.

This he did, and he took his time. He was by no means

eager to rush back and fight on the barricades. His radicalism was still more an intellectual fad than an urge for action. "We played with the problems of human life," he reflected as he looked back on that period, "for they had not become real problems for us yet, and we had not been caught in the coils of the world's affairs."

While he sat quietly and listened, his friends in the club of Indian students shouted at the tops of their voices for armed rebellion. But a few years later, most of those parlor firebrands had forgotten their revolutionary oratory. They had become judges and lawyers and military officers and were proud to hobnob with their British superiors.

In 1912 Jawaharlal passed his bar examination and shortly afterward returned to India. A little sadly he summed up the results of his education, "I have become a queer mixture of East and West, out of place everywhere, at home nowhere." He came back to the land of his ancestors an ardent Indian nationalist, but, years later, his cellmates in prison would say of him, "When he speaks in his sleep he speaks English."

5.

MANHOOD

JAWAHARLAL LANDED IN BOMBAY during the heat of summer. As befits a family of means, the Nehrus were spending the stifling hot season in the mountains. They stayed at the "hill station" (resort town) of Mussoorie, where the air is cool and the glaciers glisten in the sunlight.

Urged on by impatient letters and telegrams, Jawaharlal raced northward by fast trains. Where the railroad tracks ended, he continued on horseback.

Weeks before his announced arrival, the whole household had plunged into a whirl of activity. Servants scurried about. His mother walked with a new gleam in her eyes. Father laughed and joked continuously.

It was Motilal who first spied the lone figure on his mount slowly ascending the winding mountain path. Everybody rushed out of the house and down the path. They almost dragged him from the horse.

He embraced his parents and then Swarup, twelve years old now and almost a handsome woman in full bloom, for girls mature early under the broiling sun of India. She was already engaged to marry, by parental arrangement, of course.

"You are so thin, Jawaharji. Did you have enough to eat?" asked Rani Nehru.

"You have your sheepskin from Cambridge with you?" inquired Motilal. "When is your luggage coming?"

"What did you bring me from London?" Swarup wanted to know.

With laughter and many gestures the fledgling barrister parried the onslaught of questions. Still trying to sort them out and to answer them one by one, he was interrupted by a child's crying.

"I want to go home," wailed an unhappy little voice. "I'm hungry and thirsty."

As he looked down, Jawaharlal remembered what had been reported to him in many glowing letters from home. He lifted the girl in his arms and kissed her. "So this is the baby sister. She is quite a lady now." With this not very original remark he put her down. The very next minute he had forgotten all about her.

Krishna Nehru, born during his absence from India, had been uneasy for some time. Everybody talked only about that unknown big brother. She had felt slighted and neglected. And now this. It took Krishna many years to live down the inner hurt she had received on that day when she met Jawaharlal for the first time.

At summer's end the Nehrus returned to Allahabad, and Jawaharlal again became a member of the sumptuous household at Anand Bhawan. Dutifully he took up the practice of law before the High Court. With his father's far-reaching influence, his future seemed assured.

As was to be expected, he was not overly busy as a beginner. So he spent long hours at the club, where his colleagues made small talk about their cases while sipping cool drinks from long-stemmed glasses.

It did not take Jawaharlal long to discover that he was not really interested in being an attorney. He could have made a passable living at it, but he just was not able to work up any enthusiasm over the fine print of a mortgage contract. Fiery oratory in favor of a landowner who fought with his neighbor over the exact boundary line seemed to him quite ridiculous.

An experienced friend advised him to write a book on some legal problem. That was always a good way to get ahead in the profession. But Nehru, who proved in later years his consummate mastery of the pen, could not bring himself to delve into some obscure problem of legal reasoning.

He was in danger of being a failure. The best part about his work was that it left plenty of hours for pleasure. But the young man who had tasted the night life and the arts of London found the pleasures of a provincial town like Allahabad quite limited.

Outings into the mountains of the North or the jungles of the South were for him the only satisfying pastimes. "The call of the jungle and the mountains," he once wrote, "has always been strong within me, a dweller of cities and of plains though I am."

Such outings often took the form of hunting parties. With great zest Jawaharlal joined in the hikes through forests and glades, but when the animal was cornered and it was time to pull the trigger, he felt uneasy. He had the old Hindu reluctance to destroy life in any form, plus a humanitarian outlook gained through the study of Western philosophers. The final chapter of his hunting career was written by a little antelope that once fell, wounded to death, at his feet. It looked up at him with its big eyes full of misery and silent reproach. Nehru never again raised a gun against a living creature.

In the Western world romance is usually the great emotional experience of the young adult. Not so in the Orient. Ancient marriage customs are the last to change. Nehru wore Western clothes and thought Western thoughts, but when the question of a wife had to be faced, the parents did the selecting, and the son meekly accepted their choice.

At a religious festival Rani Nehru met a tall, slim girl of seventeen, a well-to-do merchant's daughter of the proper Kashmiri Brahmin background. Her name was Kamala. It

·was decided that she would make a good wife for twenty-six-year-old Jawaharlal, and a date in March was set for the wedding.

Preparations went on for months. Jewelers, tailors and merchants came and went all day. The date of the wedding, carefully selected by the astrologers as particularly auspicious, was *Vasanta Panchami*, which heralds the coming of spring. A week before, the Nehrus and their hundreds of guests moved to Delhi, which was the home of the bride. They traveled in a beautifully decorated special train.

In Delhi the overflow of the wedding party was housed in a tent city which resounded, day and night, with festive clamor. The women were resplendent with hundreds of tiny silver sequins sewed to their saris. Their large earrings and golden bracelets tinkled when they moved. Ballad singers, ballet dancers and dramatic troups came from afar to entertain the guests.

Then the big day arrived. To the sounds of drums and flutes the groom was conducted to the house of the bride. Jawaharlal now wore bejeweled traditional garb with an enormous glittering turban. Kamala awaited him, dressed in a red bridal sari with brilliant flowers in her dark hair. The two families sprinkled rose water on each other while from the balconies the guests showered flower petals upon them. In the courtyard the priests chanted, and the bridal couple, the ends of their clothing tied together, held hands across the sacred fire.

In 1917, the year following the marriage, a daughter, their only child, was born. She was named Indira Priyadarshani, "one whose presence gladdens the god Indra," but she was called simply Indira.

Few men have written more movingly about their beloved than Jawaharlal wrote about Kamala:

"How fortunate we were, I told her and she agreed, for though we had sometimes quarreled and grown angry with each other, we had kept that vital spark alight, and for each one of us life was always unfolding new adventure and giving fresh insight into each other."

But this abiding love was slow in budding and late in flowering. In the beginning the marriage, so noisily inaugurated, was marred by indifference and misunderstanding. Kamala became, as was the custom, a member of the Nehru household. In the bustle of Anand Bhawan it was hard to find the privacy that two young people, still strangers to each other, needed to get to know one another.

In the summer following the wedding, the whole Nehru clan traveled to Kashmir. Jawaharlal and Kamala came along, but he seemed to be more interested in mountain-climbing with his cronies than in keeping her company. His forays were quite daring. Once while crossing a fog-shrouded ice field he fell into a crevice. Only a stout rope that kept him dangling till he could be rescued prevented early widowhood for Kamala.

The young matron, who had little formal education, was rather straightforward in expressing her likes and dislikes. Combined with Jawaharlal's inherited quick temper and his intellectual sophistication, this made an explosive mixture.

Yet as the years went by their relationship grew more tender. As a dutiful Indian wife Kamala tried hard to make her husband's interests and goals her own. On the other hand, Jawaharlal's inherent kindness of heart made him soon regret any outbursts of anger, and he always made up for them.

Not many years after the marriage, it became evident that Kamala, like her mother-in-law, was of delicate health. She developed tuberculosis and had to spend a great part of her adulthood as an invalid. Her affliction drew her husband closer to her. Krishna once wrote about her brother, "In a sickroom Jawahar is an ideal nurse. His gentleness and understanding are infinite under the most trying circumstances, and his patience is unlimited."

The two most important women in his life wasted away

before his eyes in long periods of illness. This experience imprinted itself deeply upon his sensitive mind.

For some years Jawaharlal Nehru fretted uneasily in his gilded prison. He was restless. Groping and seeking, he waited for some clarion call that would pull him out of his lazy life. He felt he was only marking time.

In a vague sense he considered himself a socialist because he wanted a better deal for the underdog. But he was just an armchair reformer, far removed from real contact with the underdog.

Haltingly, as a hesitant bather first sticks only one toe into the cold creek, he began to dabble in Congress' politics. He attended some of their meetings, held periodically in different cities. Congress was still a small organization and it lacked fire and daring. "Essentially," he wrote about his first impressions, "it was a social gathering with no political excitement or tension."

Nothing was there that could compare with the fire of a Garibaldi and his red-shirted followers. Still missing was the yeast that would make the inert dough rise.

In the meantime, the bloody nightmare of the First World War descended upon the European continent. Though India was far away from the center of the blast, the shock waves extended all the way across Asia. Over a million Indians, partly volunteers and partly pressed into service, marched off to the trenches of northern France and to the desert battlefields of the Near East. Those who returned brought back a new attitude. They were unwilling to just take off their uniforms and sink back into the former stupor of village life.

All over Europe old regimes were tottering, old boundaries wiped out. Czechs and Poles were demanding independence. Louder and louder rose the question, "What about India?"

At first the Indian upper classes meekly supported the British war effort. Rani and Kamala knitted bandages and warm garments for the boys at the front, and Jawaharlal applied to join the Indian Defense Force. This was a volunteer corps, with recruiting stations in all large cities, organized by a committee of respected Indian leaders.

But the more persistent Radicals gathered secretly in homes and parks and rejoiced at the news of German victories, not because they liked the Germans, but because they were gratified to see the self-assured British masters humbled.

As the war progressed the Western powers suffered setback after setback. Things were not going well in Flanders and in the Mediterranean. At times the situation looked quite desperate. India was called upon to furnish even more manpower and also more food and cotton for the embattled armies.

Partly to get better cooperation from Indians, a Liberal government in London decided on mild reforms for the crown colony. For the first time Indians were appointed to the advisory council of the viceroy. In the various Indian provinces candidates of native stock could now be elected to the legislative assemblies and even fill the posts of ministers in the provincial governments. But the governors of the provinces, who were always Britishers, and particularly the viceroy in New Delhi retained the final say-so on all vital matters.

The Moderates in Congress expressed satisfaction with the reforms. The Radicals scorned them as worthless. To them they looked like skimpy bones thrown disdainfully on the ground to pacify growling dogs.

The arguments in Congress over the value of the reforms found their echo at Anand Bhawan. Motilal welcomed the piecemeal program as a step in the right direction. Jawaharlal espoused complete independence. He also argued that administrative changes were of little value unless they were linked to social reforms in depth. Freedom from hunger was as essential as freedom from political bondage.

And if England was not willing to grant all the demands? "Then," countered Jawaharlal, remembering Garibaldi's saber-swinging band, "we must take stronger action."

They debated, the son standing by his point of view even when the father's temper waxed hot. The days of filial submissiveness were coming to an end. With deep shock, servants and family members listened to the frequently loud and sometimes bitter quarrels between the older and the younger Nehru.

Jawaharlal's dedication to the nationalist cause received a powerful boost when he came under the spell of the poetess Sairojini Naidu, the "Nightingale of India." In her rousing speeches, this remarkable woman contrasted the listless and helpless India of the present with the glory of her past. "Oust the British," was her fervent battle cry, and it was taken up by a growing band of disciples.

History was on the side of the Radicals. Their cause was greatly helped by the stupidity of many British officials who, despite all the good intentions in London, insisted on treating the "natives" with a cold contempt that made the blood of nationalists boil.

Even Moderates now became uneasy. Their deep admiration of things European took a tumble, especially after the great war had so recently demonstrated that Europeans could be wrong and also that they could be beaten.

The curtain was about to rise on Jawaharlal Nehru's real life drama. Long enough had he been a passive onlooker. He yearned for action. He was burning to submerge his individual self in an all-encompassing movement.

In 1915 he managed a fund drive to assist Indians in South Africa who suffered under a vicious system of racial discrimination. Then he joined the Home Rule League. This name revived memories of the movement that fought for Irish independence. Its leader was the widely revered Annie Besant, Irish by birth and Indian by choice. For many years she had also been the spiritual head of the theosophical

cult to which Jawaharlal had briefly belonged in his boyhood.

The cry of home rule sounded loudly across the country.
It became a cry of fury at the news that seventy-year-old
Mrs. Besant had been arrested as a troublemaker.

The indignation over this and similar events caused Jawaharlal to overcome the last obstacle that stood between him
and active politics. This obstacle was his deeply ingrained
shyness and his reluctance to let himself go and swim with
the crowd. Political work consisted then mainly of talking
in public.

It was a sweltering evening in 1915. In a stuffy hall a meeting was in progress. It had been called to protest the muzzling
of the Indian press by a new government order. The speeches
droned on endlessly, and the crowd grew restless.

Jawaharlal was sitting near the platform. He squirmed in
his uncomfortable seat. They don't know how to talk to the
simple man in the street, he thought. Big phrases, long-
winded constitutional arguments: that's not what the shop-
keeper or the railroad clerk want to hear.

Suddenly his hand was up in the air. The chairman, who
had never heard him speak before, nodded to him in astonishment. Jawaharlal stood behind the lectern. His throat felt
constricted, and pearls of perspiration trickled down his
cheeks. He almost dashed back to his seat, into the protective anonymity of the crowd, but that would have been
the ultimate in embarrassment.

He began in an uncertain, high-pitched voice:

"Friends—let me tell you—er—about my days in London
—er—There is a big park, Hyde Park. Many people walk
there to relax, people like you. Children play under its trees.
Often somebody begins to speak, and listeners gather around
him. They applaud or they argue with him. He may say
that the government is bad or that the king has done wrong.
If anybody tries to harm him, a policeman protects him—"

In the audience the noise of coughing had stopped. All eyes were glued to the handsome face behind the lectern. Here was somebody telling a simple story, and they all wanted to hear how it went on. The speaker sensed the attention of his listeners. His voice became calmer, and his features relaxed. He continued with the self-assurance of a grownup talking to a group of children:

"—Prevent an Englishman from expressing himself freely at Hyde Park or anywhere else, and the whole nation will scream in protest. Forbid an English newspaper to write as it pleases, and the government will shake in its foundations. But the same Englishmen suppress our newspapers and jail our editors when they do as their English colleagues do. Is this fair?"

"No, no, no," they shouted. Neighbors nudged each other and smiled in agreement.

"Can what is right in London be wrong in Delhi or in Allahabad?" continued the speaker who had now shed every trace of uncertainty.

The chorus of No's was even louder now, and it was underscored by tumultuous hand-clapping.

"The difference is that England is a free country and we are not. When we will be free, then our policemen will protect our rights. We don't tell Englishmen or Frenchmen how to run their country. Why should anybody tell us? They say, 'You are not able to run your own affairs,' but India is much older than England. We have a right to make our own mistakes. The British have made plenty in their time—"

They interrupted him many times with their cheers, and when he had finished they jumped to their feet and waved their arms. Nehru stood with his head lowered, not quite knowing what to do next. The chairman stepped up to him, embraced him and soundly kissed him on both cheeks.

For Indians this was the expected sign of great admiration and thankfulness, but the Harrow and Cambridge man, schooled in the Anglo-Saxon reluctance to display emotion, could have sunk through the floor in embarrassment.

The good chairman was probably moved to such a sentimental gesture not so much by the superior quality of Nehru's speech as by the fact that it had been made at all. The son of a prominent, widely respected family had come out of his luxurious isolation and publicly committed himself to active work for India's cause. From now on he could be counted upon to contribute not only his time and his vocal chords, but mainly—himself.

6.

MAHATMA

JAWAHARLAL WAS PLAINLY BORED, and so were most of the other delegates to the annual Congress meeting of 1916. As always, the session had opened with three polite cheers for the king. Now resolutions were introduced and amendments to the resolutions. Speakers argued over fine points of constitutional law, using long scholarly words and quoting extensively from learned authors.

He had come with a feeling of urgency, ready to lend a hand to exciting tasks. But all he saw around him were portly gentlemen in morning coats and striped trousers conversing with each other or scanning the papers for news of the latest horse races and polo matches.

Drowsily his shoulders hunched forward, and his eyes closed. "How in the world," he wondered, "can such people lead us in a great struggle? Am I wasting my time here?"

Suddenly he was sitting up straight in his armchair. He cupped a hand over his left ear to hear better. His neighbors on both sides had abandoned their morning papers. Delegates rushed by him to stand in the aisles before the platform.

The chairman had acknowledged a bespectacled little man with a spare body and a graying mustache. He was nude except for a loincloth.

"Who's this?" whispered a stout man on Jawaharlal's right. "A beggar from the street corner?"

He was annoyed by the interruption, but answered politely,

"The chairman introduced him as a Mr. Gandhi. I read something about him the other day. He was a great success in South Africa."

Mohandas Gandhi pushed the lectern out of the way and squatted on the floor of the dais with his heels drawn up to his thighs. Ears strained to follow his words spoken in a quiet voice:

"Take off those garments. Dress like the peasant. Only with his help can we be free. No amount of speeches will make us fit for self-government. It is only our conduct that will make us deserving of it."

A murmur of shock rose from the floor.

Jawaharlal shifted uneasily in his seat. What did this strange character in beggar's garb want from them? What had peasants to do with politics? Politics was for those who understood it and could afford it.

"Strip yourselves of your valuables," continued Gandhi in the manner of a teacher admonishing his sulking pupils, "and hold them in trust for your countrymen in India. Our salvation can come only through the peasant. Neither the lawyers, nor the doctors, nor the rich landlords are going to secure it."

"This man is insane," grumbled a merchant.

"He doesn't know anything about politics, that's obvious," complained a lawyer. "What is he doing here?"

"He should go and speak at a temple. That's where he belongs, not in a political meeting."

Gandhi spoke on. He seemed to know none of the rules by which the political game is customarily played. Instead of citing parliamentary acts and cabinet decisions he quoted from the Upanishad (oo.pan'y.shad) the sacred book in which the ancient Hindu sages have traced man's way to absolute perfection. Like the Hebrew prophets of old he called for a moral renewal. He pleaded for a spiritual crusade.

Jawaharlal left the meeting deeply stirred and very confused. This man reminded him of the ascetics sitting at the religious shrines, their naked bodies smeared with ashes. How was he to carry the banner of liberation?

Nothing in the history books offered any parallels. When Garibaldi's rebels or the Irish nationalists wanted freedom, they took up arms and fought. They did not take off their garments and mumble pious words of love and peace.

Yet Jawaharlal could not shake off the spell of those quiet words. There was some inexplicable fascination in them. For hours he walked through the noisy streets pondering the question, "Who really was Gandhi?" What he knew about him was common knowledge.

Mohandas K. Gandhi had also studied in London for the bar, but the spirit of the West had remained alien to him. His Indian soul had shed it as an oily surface sheds the water.

After returning from England he had practiced law in his home state. A case called him to South Africa where a sizable Indian minority had settled. He had meant to be away a few short months, but stayed for twenty-two years, leading his countrymen there in a spectacular fight against legal enslavement and racial suppression. Now, forty-nine years old, he was back—a hero. The haughty South African authorities had been forced, after long hesitation, to negotiate with him and had then removed some of the worst injustices. And all this had been achieved without bloodshed. Nobody was assassinated, no bombs were thrown. By example and by urgent persuasion he had converted his people from shrinking, fear-smitten creatures into proud men and women who asserted their rights peacefully, but bravely.

Now he was back in India. His fame had preceded him. Wherever he went, the common people were acclaiming him as the *Mahatma* (ma.hät'ma), the Great Soul. Only rarely had a living person been called by this revered title.

The conflict raging in Jawaharlal's mind kept him awake most of the night and many nights thereafter. The Mahatma's insistence on poverty and simplicity was hard to take. Why was that so important? Why the denial of the good things in life? Religion should be kept out of politics, thought Nehru, the freethinker.

And yet, there was a curious strength in Gandhi's plain, unadorned language. Was he a fool or a great leader? Jawaharlal was determined to find out.

Gandhi's approach to life was rooted in ancient Indian thought. He wanted a return to sacred old customs. Modern innovations seemed to him flippant and unimportant.

But Gandhi's religion was not the superstitious mumbo-jumbo of astrologers and diviners. He rejected what was outworn in Hinduism and shone his spotlight on the ideas that were great and eternal. His basic creed was that all life is holy and worthy and must be respected. This was the root of his insistence on nonviolence in any conflict, political or otherwise.

He taught that never, not even in the white heat of struggle for power, must moral precepts be forgotten. The means must always be worthy of the end. If one had to fight, the fighting should be done without physical harm. Enmity must be directed only against causes, not against the persons who represent them.

Fine words, thought Jawaharlal, but thoroughly impractical. But as he observed the Mahatma in action, he discovered to his amazement a shrewd mind and an iron will in the emaciated body. And Gandhi was not a cold kill-joy of a saint, but a thoroughly human person full of smiles and humor. "There were no rough edges or sharp corners about him," admitted Nehru, "no trace of vulgarity or commonness, in which, unhappily, our classes excel."

How effective was such strategy under fire? Jawaharlal knew, of course, of Gandhi's success in South Africa. But this was India, not Africa. He had to be convinced that the Mahatma's road was the right one for his native country.

The opportunity arose soon.

During the same Congress session a poor peasant approached Gandhi. "I am from Champaran, and we want you to come to our district."

Gandhi hesitated, but the peasant courier kept squatting patiently at the door of his lodgings till he agreed to travel to the remote district which lay in the foothills of the Himalaya. There, in the indigo plantations, the rent of the sharecroppers had recently been raised, bringing their families to the edge of starvation. When they refused to work under those conditions, they were beaten, their houses looted, their cattle impounded.

Jawaharlal was burning with curiosity as Gandhi began to investigate. Eagerly he scanned the papers for news from those wretched Himalayan villages. Dimly he felt that history was in the making there.

The local British authorities ordered Gandhi to leave the district. He refused and was arrested. At his trial he declared, "I cannot obey laws which are unjust and immoral nor the authorities who enforce such laws. I am prepared to endure the punishment provided rather than to bow to injustice." He was polite and friendly to the judge, for whom such behavior in court was a completely new experience. The jurist could not help treating the accused in turn with deep respect.

Following events from afar, Jawaharlal began to perceive a pattern in Gandhi's baffling behavior, a pattern which fascinated him more with every passing day.

The case was dropped. Thousands of peasants who had ringed the courthouse carried the Mahatma off in triumph. He continued his work. The moral indignation with which he announced his findings eventually shamed the authorities into action. The rent increases were canceled, and Champaran became a cherished word all over India.

The Mahatma went on, by third-class railroad coach, by bullock cart and on foot, to other rural districts and repeated his triumphs.

Jawaharlal was convinced. The test of practicability had

been applied. An unarmed population can become the most fearsome adversary when its campaigns become crusades and martyrdom is welcomed.

After successful trials here and there, Gandhi raised the banner of mass civil disobedience all over the nation. By that time, the younger Nehru had decided to march behind it.

One morning, while staying with a friend in Madras, Gandhi announced to his host, "Last night the idea came to me in a dream that we should call on the country to observe a general *hartal.*"

A *hartal,* deeply rooted in Hindu tradition, is a combination of religious festival, fast day and general strike. People assemble in open places to receive messages from their leaders.

But this *hartal* was not an end in itself, sensational though it was. Gandhi had only designed it as the opening signal for a long-range course of action which he called *satyagraha* (sut'ya.gru'ha). *Satyagraha* became the basic weapon of Gandhi's strategy. He had experimented with it in South Africa, but it reached its full flowering in his own homeland.

As Gandhi had instructed him, Jawaharlal proclaimed the message of *satyagraha* all over his home district. In speech after speech he called on the citizens of Allahabad and its environs to take their children out of English schools, to shun British courts, to boycott elections to the legislatures and to refuse any kind of British honors.

He passed along Gandhi's powerful call for the complete boycott of British goods. Enthusiastic volunteers in large numbers manned the picket lines which he posted outside stores selling English woolens and English liquors. Among the pickets were his own wife, Kamala, and his sisters Swarup and Krishna.

Indian manufacturing was still quite insignificant. How then should Indians procure what they needed if they were to shun the products of English factories?

"Rely on your own resources," counseled Gandhi. "Get out your old spinning wheels. Make your own clothes."

He himself included several hours of spinning in his daily routine. The old-fashioned spinning wheel became the symbol of Gandhi's movement and *khadi*, the rough homespun garment, its unofficial uniform.

Jawaharlal felt a strange elation such as he had never known before. It was as if the call for volunteers was personally directed at him. "Here at last was a way out of the tangle," he wrote, "a method of action which was straight and open and possibly effective. I was afire with enthusiasm."

He was ready to join the Mahatma, as from time immemorial religious disciples have joined their *guru,* their spiritual master. This meant giving up his career, his whole established pattern of life. Following the Mahatma was not a part-time job, not even an occupation in the usual sense. It meant complete submission under a discipline as rigid and austere as in a monastic order.

Jawaharlal knew it could also mean a complete and probably violent break with his father.

Motilal Nehru was aware of Gandhi's course. How could he help it? He had been a prominent member of Congress long before the Mahatma burst upon the scene. He had observed how the derisive laughter of the delegates turned into admiration, how they finally all succumbed to his magnetic personality. He watched him take over the unquestioned leadership of Congress.

Motilal recognized the iron will behind the humble exterior, the will of a born commander who insisted, "So long as you keep me as your leader, you must accept my conditions, you must accept dictatorship. But that dictatorship will always be subject to your good will and to your acceptance and to your cooperation. The moment you have enough of me, throw me out, trample on me, and I shall not complain."

Grudgingly at first, Motilal could not help admiring how,

under Gandhi's magic spell, Congress turned from a sleepy debating society into a vigorous mass movement. But everything in him rebelled against the style of life the Mahatma had chosen for himself and for his assistants.

Fighting—yes, he could appreciate its thrill, especially when it was a question of fighting with words, with ideas, as in the courtroom. But passive resistance? There was no personal satisfaction in it, he thought. The prospect of going to jail and being beaten by the police without lifting a finger sounded rather dismal to him. And besides, how could this bring victory?

Yet Motilal had to admit that the traditional political weapons had become dull and ineffective. The new dignity and quiet strength the Indian masses were beginning to show under Gandhi's leadership impressed him greatly.

In his soul raged a terrible conflict. The arguments between father and son became louder and more frequent as the father became less sure of his own stand, and the son more certain that he had found the right way.

One evening they argued more vehemently than usual. Motilal lost his self-control.

"Get out of this house." He shouted so loudly that the crystalware on the table tingled. "You fool. I won't have any insolent beggar give me lessons. As long as you eat my bread you obey my orders."

Jawaharlal's face darkened. He too had a quick temper, but he suppressed a sharp reply. He was about to turn on his heels and walk out of his father's house forever, but at that moment a small cool hand slipped gently into his. His head turned, and a pair of dark, luminous eyes looked straight into his as if to say, "Be calm. You still have me. You always will. I, Kamala, understand you."

Motilal gazed at the handsome couple before him engrossed in each other. Embarrassment turned his face a bright red. "Oh, well. Forget it," he huffed. "You're of age. Do as

your conscience tells you." And he stomped out of the
room.

For days afterward, Jawaharlal wandered sleeplessly about
the grounds of Anand Bhawan. His mind was tormented,
torn between his duty as a son and his eagerness to dedicate
himself with complete abandon to the cause of his *guru*.
Slowly he strolled through the gardens and orchards.

One night, as he dragged himself back into the house,
he saw light in his father's bedroom. He tiptoed to the door,
which was slightly ajar. He was uncertain. Perhaps now was
a good time to talk and settle this thing once and for all.

He halted at the door and peered into the room. There
was his father, also sleepless, pacing from wall to wall like
a big caged animal. His high forehead was in a deep frown,
and, from time to time, a sigh issued from his lips.

Jawaharlal knew what was in Motilal's mind. An overpowering love for the grand old man welled up in the son.

Then he saw a strange thing. His father switched off the
electric lamp, but enough moonlight was streaming through
the open windows so that he could see Motilal standing
for a moment hesitatingly before the open bed. Then he
turned away from it, as if he had just made a very weighty
decision, and lay down on the hard floor.

Jawaharlal stormed into the room full of anxiety.

"What is the matter, Father? Are you ill? I'll call the
servants."

"You, Jawahar?" Motilal sounded embarrassed. "What are
you doing here? Don't call anybody. I'm all right."

"I was walking in the garden thinking about our last
argument. I have to apologize for having lost my temper
earlier in the evening. But why are you lying on the floor?"

"This was not for anybody else to see. Sounds silly now."

"Silly? It looked as if you had fainted or something."

"Well, if you must know, I'm still trying to decide whether
to give you my blessing when you join the Mahatma, for

I feel, with or without my blessing, you will eventually join him. I know it will mean prison for you, and so I thought I would see for myself how it feels to sleep on a hard prison cot or on the floor of the cell. Perhaps after knowing first-hand I could make a wiser decision."

With tears streaming down his face Jawaharlal embraced his father. Then he walked silently to his room.

Next morning Motilal sent an invitation to Gandhi, and the Mahatma, sensing the reason, came immediately to Anand Bhawan. For many hours the two elderly men re-mained closeted, opening their hearts to each other.

Then Jawaharlal was summoned into the room. His heart beat a staccato as he entered. He knew that he had been the topic of this strange conference. His father and his *guru,* the two great influences upon his life, must have come to a decision. He was sure that the Mahatma's irresistible charm had won out.

Gandhi flashed his famous smile. "I have talked with your father, Jawaharlalji. He is beginning to see the value of *satyagraha.* But," he raised a bony finger in the gesture of friendly warning, "don't hasten matters. A good son must never cause his father any pain. Give him time. It is not easy for him."

Jawaharlal was disappointed, but he could not very well disregard the wishes of these two men. He knew that Gandhi needed his help, but even under the pressure of intense political activity, a son's traditional duty of obedience to his father took precedence in the Mahatma's way of thinking. There was nothing to do but wait.

He did not have to wait long.

The pace of the independence movement quickened by the hour. *Satyagraha Day* had been a resounding success. In Jawaharlal's own province the response had exceeded all expectations. Never again would India be the same.

But the stern command of nonviolence was not obeyed everywhere. Here and there exuberant mobs went out of control. Police and soldiers responded with bullets. Wholesale reprisals were ordered. Over parts of India descended the stifling pall of martial law. Armed force tried to get a strangle hold on the awakening country.

This was the final signal for the whole Nehru family.

Jawaharlal hung up his attorney's robe, never to put it on again. As a novice enters a monastery, he dressed himself in white homespun and joined Gandhi's shock troops of non-violent civil disobedience.

Not a religious person by nature or training, he fell so strongly under the Mahatma's spell that he gave up many habits of his former life of ease. He did not touch any meat. He shunned smoking and alcoholic beverages and became accustomed to the hard benches of third-class railroad coaches.

Still he could not always agree with the Mahatma's ideas and with his strategy.

"Why all these fast days and prayer meetings?" he argued with his leader. "Can't we keep politics apart from religion?"

"You may be able to keep them separate, but not the simple people." The Mahatma smiled. He was never offended. "You don't have to fast and pray with us if you don't feel the need. Stick to your books. But why not read the *Bhagavad Gita* sometimes?"

Jawaharlal did, and he was deeply stirred by the philosophy contained in the ancient Hindu epic, even though he discounted its stories as children's fables.

He also felt at a loss to understand the master's love of the spinning wheel. Gandhi's ideal was a rural self-sufficient society with few and simple needs. On the other hand, Nehru dreamed of a modern industrialized India. Intricate machinery held a lifelong fascination for him.

"Gandhiji was a very difficult person to understand," he wrote. "Sometimes his language was almost incomprehensible to the average modern."

But this gap between the rationalistic and the mystic mind did not impair Jawaharlal's unwavering devotion to his *guru*.

Even when he disagreed he submitted to the older man's wisdom on all matters of practical politics. In most instances, Gandhi's judgment turned out to be correct. Jawaharlal learned from the Mahatma to identify with the peasant, the poor of the city, the Untouchable. He learned to fight without hating.

From the beginning of their relationship, one point in the Mahatma's program struck a particularly sympathetic response in Jawaharlal's heart: the emphasis on religious unity. The nationalist movement embraced Indians of all creeds. Moslems and Hindus marched side by side under the banner of *satyagraha*.

A new all-consuming force had entered his life. He now had a clear goal and a sense of personal commitment. He said, "So great was this personal satisfaction that even a possibility of failure did not count for much, for such failure could only be temporary."

And Motilal? Not only was there no break between father and son, but the older Nehru, proud, imperial Motilal, chose, after a time, to follow in the footsteps of his son. Their roles had been reversed. Kamala, Jawaharlal's two sisters, and even his ailing mother—they all were now active campaigners in the cause of the Mahatma. The charmer had done a thorough job on the Nehru family.

Motilal, too, hung his expertly tailored suits into the closet and put on *khadi*. Luxurious Anand Bhawan was turned over to Congress and became its headquarters. The family moved into more modest quarters across the street. Tearfully the servants packed up the Dresden china, the damask table linen, the carpets and oil paintings, all to be sold or auctioned off.

Jawaharlal and the members of his family were soon to find out how hard the floors of prison cells were.

7.

THE SUFFERING AND THE POOR

JAWAHARLAL WAS NOW a full-time Congress worker. He served his political apprenticeship as a kind of secretary to Gandhi and, on special occasions, to other veteran Congress leaders.

In the spring of 1919 he accompanied a Congress committee to the city of Amritsar in the Punjab region. Something horrible had occurred there, but what it was remained a mystery for several weeks. The city was isolated. Travel and mail service were suspended. Only wild rumors filtered through the tight censorship. Congress was, of course, greatly alarmed and decided to carry out its own investigation. What they found out was worse than the rumors.

General Michael O. Dyer, the lieutenant governor of the Amritsar area, was a tough disciplinarian of the old school. For him the independence movement was nothing but mischief caused by impertinent native rabble-rousers who had to be taught a lesson. He had recently introduced public floggings for demonstrators, a form of punishment which, so he thought, would frighten all the local followers of Gandhi into meek submission.

In defiance of his orders, a large but peaceful crowd assembled one morning to protest the new humiliation. The meeting took place at Jallianwalla Bagh, a public park in the heart of the city, almost completely surrounded by walls which formed the boundaries of adjoining houses. There was only one exit wide enough to allow a few persons to pass at a time.

Told about the assembly, General Dyer ordered a company of soldiers to the spot. They posted themselves at the entrance and opened fire without warning. The shooting continued till the ammunition was exhausted. The result: nearly four hundred dead and about twelve hundred wounded. Many of the corpses were found piled against the walls. The soldiers must have aimed their fire directly at those who had tried to climb to safety.

An official inquiry was held, and General Dyer testified. Jawaharlal who witnessed the hearing was deeply shocked as he observed the British officer's self-righteous arrogance. Far from regretting the needless bloodbath, the general boasted, "They deserved a lesson. They had it coming for a long time. I had them at my mercy. I should have left Amritsar in smoking ruins, but I took pity on those miserable wretches."

Even in London the Amritsar affair caused grave repercussions. Shame and regret were loudly expressed in parliamentary circles and strongly voiced in the newspapers. In the wake of public indignation General Dyer was retired from active duty, but otherwise he remained free from any penalty. His one-track mind probably never grasped the fact that at Amritsar he had lost India for his king.

In Jawaharlal's heart there was a feeling of disenchantment with British justice, which he had learned to consider one of mankind's brightest accomplishments. Saddened and grim he went back to his regular duties. But an even greater shock was in store for him.

Busy with Congress work, he was unable to spend the following summer in the mountains as had been his custom in earlier years. Those sultry June days in Allahabad brought destiny to his doorstep. He met the *kisan*.

The *kisan* is the Indian peasant. His mud hut stood perhaps only a few miles from the city, yet he might as well have lived on a different planet, so completely ignorant of his joys and woes were the city dwellers. No teacher taught about the rural situation. No newspaper reported it. Nobody showed the least bit of interest.

One morning Jawaharlal learned that some two hundred peasants had walked fifty miles to Allahabad and were squatting on the bank of the Jumna River. Being of a curious nature, he went there to find out what it was all about.

Immediately he was surrounded by half-naked, barefoot men, waving their thin, knotted arms and shouting at the same time:

"Come, sahib, we beg you. Come with us to the village."

"See how the landlords treat us."

Jawaharlal did not know what to do. He wanted to get away without hurting them. "I am not the government. I can't do anything for you. You must go to the officials."

But they insisted:

"The officials won't listen to us."

"Come with us. We want you to know."

"The landlords will punish us for going to the city. Come, protect us."

"We heard you belong to those who are fighting for better days in India."

"Come with us—"

Jawaharlal relented. He summoned a few friends, and two days later was on his way. What he saw was an overpowering revelation. "A new picture of India seemed to rise before me," he confessed. "naked, starving, crushed and utterly miserable."

He found the *kisan* enmeshed in a vicious sharecropping system that put him at the complete mercy of landlords, moneylenders and bribed officials. The rent was exorbitant. In addition, the landlord exacted special levies when his daughter got married or when he sent his son away to college. Receipts for rent paid were never issued. When the peasant got too far behind in his payments he had to turn

to the moneylender, who charged outrageously high interests. Then followed eviction from land and house. A great
number of the *kisans* Jawaharlal met were landless.

Lack of nourishment and ignorance about health care
kept them weak and listless. In their cringing fear they had
allowed themselves for generations to be kicked and beaten
by their masters and by the police, who always took the side
of their exploiters.

Yet, Jawaharlal could not fail to notice that a fresh wind
was blowing through the countryside. In his simplicity the
peasant was dimly aware that some efforts were under way
to lighten his burden. It was all too involved for his un-
trained mind, but there was no mistaking the excitement
that swept through the drab villages.

At times somebody would raise the cry, "*Sita-Ram.*" It
was an ancient supplication to the god Rama and his spouse,
Sita. The shout would ring through the village, "*Sita-Ra-
a-am.*" It was repeated across the fields, a signal similar to
the drumbeat in the African bush. At the cry whole villages
would empty out. By the thousands the peasants would
stream to giant meetings hoping to hear a prophecy of better
times ahead.

Thus they came to hear the words of the young Brahmin
from Allahabad. "I was filled with shame and sorrow," he
reported about these impromptu meetings, "shame at my
easygoing life and our petty politics of the city which ignored
this vast multitude of seminaked sons and daughters of
India."

He spent three days in the villages, returned to Allahabad
and then went out again. He traveled by car, but there were
no roads. Often when the automobile got stuck in the soft
dirt, it was bodily lifted out by scores of willing hands.
Hundreds of peasants built temporary roads across the fields
so that the car could pass into the interior. Finally Jawaharlal
realized that the only truly effective way to reach the *kisan*
was to travel on foot.

So he began to trudge along the byways of India under the blinding June sun with a towel wrapped around his head for protection. His white skin took on a deep tan. Soon he realized with surprise that physical discomfort had ceased to bother him.

In the semidarkness of the huts with their cots of hemp rope, and by the slimy village wells, Nehru experienced the meaning of poverty which had been so totally absent from his own way of life. He had found the real India, and he was to remain its champion from then on. He continued his visits to the villages year after year. Soon the rural masses began to worship him as a kind of savior with a Gandhi cap.

In the company of the *kisans* he lost the last traces of his old shyness. "They taught me how to speak in public," he acknowledged. He learned to address them in the simplest terms, as a schoolmaster speaks to his first-grade pupils. Through unending practice he became fluent in Hindustani, the native dialect.

Since those early days in the villages Nehru's manner of speech remained casual and informal, a kind of heart-to-heart talk with the feeling of on-the-spot improvisation. It became his trademark in public life.

Sometimes he spoke to a few dozen listeners at a railroad stop. Or his audience might number tens of thousands. Often his voice did not carry to the far edge of the crowd, but it did not seem to matter. They were satisfied to hear his voice, even to get a glimpse of him. Their pinched faces glowed with excitement, and their eyes glistened with hope. They came to meet him with gifts of fruit and flower garlands and addressed him, to his embarrassment, in such terms as, "O Jewel of India," "O Embodiment of Sacrifice."

Jawaharlal became the indispensable Congress contact with the man in the street and in the field. None of his colleagues, with the sole exception of Gandhi, could establish rapport with the masses the way he could.

As the peasant needed to be won over to the Congress

ideas, Congress needed to be made aware of the peasant. Jawaharlal became the spokesman of a faction that demanded more attention to social reforms, to the breaking up of special privileges and monopolies. This group was tagged the "left." From then on Congress meetings resounded with the heated debates between right and left.

In the meantime, Nehru's crusades into the countryside were beginning to bear fruit. A new attitude became noticeable. The peasants seemed to walk straighter. Losing their abject fear, they learned to act collectively. When a tenant was ejected from his holdings, no other *kisan* came forward to take his place. At times, masses of peasants forced magistrates to release their arrested leaders simply by surrounding the courthouse.

The authorities became extremely nervous about the new spirit in the villages which threatened the whole established social system. Gandhi and Nehru taught the idea of nonviolence, but they were not always well understood. When peasants made angry gestures against their masters, the police were quick to retaliate with brutality.

In one district the peasants fell upon a landlord's property, looting and destroying. Ironically, they thought it was the Mahatma's wish. Servants of another landlord had played upon their ignorance, saying that Gandhi wanted them to plunder the rival's possessions. The simple creatures never grasped the inconsistency of breaking into the landlord's house with lively shouts of *"Mahatma Gandhi ki jai"* ("Victory to Mahatma Gandhi").

When Nehru heard of the looting he rushed to the scene. The rallying cry went out, and in a few hours some six thousand persons had assembled.

He berated them in harsh words: "You have betrayed the cause of the Mahatma. You have brought shame to our creed of nonviolence. I want those who have taken part in the looting to raise their hands and publicly confess their guilt."

The magic of his personality was so powerful and their

trust so great that two dozen hesitant hands actually went up.

Nehru regretted his rash words of that moment almost immediately. It was easy for him to be self-righteous, but he had forgotten that police agents were always at his heels. The names of the poor devils were taken down, and soon they were under arrest.

The secret agents detailed to shadow him on his rural journeys often had a hard time keeping up with him. One young detective, obviously not well acquainted with the Indian countryside, turned up in patent leather pumps. He felt so miserable trotting through the stubble fields that he begged the object of his surveillance to slow down. Nehru saw no particular reason to oblige the police. His nice shoes shredded and his feet a mass of cuts and blisters, the poor fellow had to abandon his assignment. In the personnel files of the Indian police his record was marred by an ugly black mark.

8.

CROWN PRINCE

"SIMON, GO BACK," chanted the crowd. "Si-mon go-back. Si-mon go-back." With his full lungpower Jawaharlal joined in the staccato shouts that echoed from the Lucknow railroad station. He had led the mighty procession, and now the demonstrators stood in front of the terminal building in a tightly packed human wall waving banners and placards. Some carried black flags that hung limply in the quiet air. Smaller groups still trickled from the side streets and merged into the main body.

"Simon, go back." For many demonstrators those were the only English words they knew, and they chanted them over and over.

Jawaharlal had to smile as he thought of poor Mr. Simon, the object of all this inhospitable noise. The gentleman was not really a monster, but a fairly harmless British politician. He was the head of the Simon Commission, which the British government had dispatched to India in 1919 to see how earlier reforms were working out and to make recommendations about further changes. This did not sound very vicious, but the Indian National Congress resented the fact that no Indian was on the commission. "Shall the fate of our country," asked the nationalists, "be entirely weighed and charted by foreigners?"

The call had gone out to boycott the Simon Commission. To the dismay of local officials, the traveling gentlemen were met everywhere by hostile, yet peaceful, crowds with black

78

flags inviting them to shake the dust of India from their feet.

"The police. They're coming on horses," shouted a young man in white *khadi* clothes.

"Let them come," called Jawaharlal loudly. "Remember the Mahatma's instructions. Don't give an inch, but don't fight back. Don't raise your hand against the police no matter what."

Now they were on them, swarms of mounted police. The horses galloped straight at the human wall, then reared at the last moment before the impact. For a split second Jawaharlal saw two sharp hoofs poised high above his head. Then his face and shoulders were struck by blows of the *lathees* (lä′tēs), the metal-tipped bamboo staffs of the police.

The assault was terrific. Slowly the ranks of demonstrators fell back.

Suddenly Nehru stood alone on the big plaza, and the furious blows reined on him from all sides. He staggered drunkenly, but did not retreat. Through him raged an intense urge to hit back at his tormentors. "But," he reported afterward, "long training and discipline held, and I did not raise a hand except to protect my face from blows."

He received a terrible whipping that seemed to last for hours, but in reality was over in a few seconds. Fearing for his life, some young followers dashed out from the ranks and dragged him back into the protective anonymity of the main body of people.

Word spread that the train carrying the Simon Commission had arrived. But to avoid the welcome prepared for them, the Englishmen had been spirited away through a side entrance. There was no further point in keeping up the demonstration. The procession made its way back to Congress headquarters, where it disbanded. Jawaharlal staggered along, bleeding, his body covered with welts and bruises.

This was a typical day in the career of a nonviolent rebel.

On another occasion Nehru visited the territory of the Maharaja of Nabha, which was actually ruled by the maharaja's British adviser. Jawaharlal came with two other congressional workers to investigate stories of atrocities com-mitted by the police against a religious minority, the Sikhs (sēks).

At the border of Nabha the three travelers were ordered not to enter the maharaja's realm. When they persisted they were arrested. They were handcuffed together, one prisoner's left wrist to the other's right, and a chain, attached to the handcuffs, was held by a policeman. So they were marched through the little border town and then taken by train to the state's capital. Still handcuffed they were left, for three days, in an indescribably filthy jail. As they tried to sleep on the floor, rats and mice scurried over their faces.

Then followed a trial for conspiracy that was a complete farce. The accused were not allowed to defend themselves nor even to know the exact nature of the charges. The lawyer in Jawaharlal recognized immediately that the judge knew nothing of laws and even less of court procedures.

They were sentenced to two years in prison each, but on the same night the superintendent of the jail came to their cell and showed them an order from higher up, obviously prepared in advance of the trial, suspending the sentences and expelling them from Nabha territory immediately. An hour later they were on a train bringing them back to friendlier regions. For some time thereafter they were plagued by a souvenir from this adventure—typhoid fever.

Attending to his more conventional duties, Jawaharlal spent his days and often also his nights in airless offices and at lengthy committee meetings. Old contacts and friends were neglected. He had no time for books and newspapers, except as their contents referred to the movement. His family saw very little of him.

But the masses cheered his every word as if it were the divine truth. Throngs of admirers followed him through the streets. Thousands came to his home in Allahabad, as tourists visit museums and shrines, making ordinary privacy a thing of the past. They peered at him through windows and from balconies. Everybody wanted a glimpse of *Panditji* (pun'dit'je —wise man.)

Did all this hero-worship make Nehru conceited? He has himself pondered this question carefully, as he always is his most merciless critic. "Only a saint, perhaps," he admitted, "or an inhuman monster could survive all this, unscathed and unaffected, and I can place myself in neither of these categories."

The members of his own family enjoyed teasing him about all the extravagant praise. Also as a kind of antidote, Kamala or one of his sisters would ask at the breakfast table, "O Jewel of India, please pass the butter." Not to be outdone, little Indira piped up with something like, "O Embodiment of Sacrifice, you're dripping jam on the tablecloth."

Jawaharlal always joined in the general laughter. Only his mother remained stern, and her eyes showed disapproval. She wanted her important son taken seriously, even in the family circle.

The younger Nehru was indeed the rising star on the nationalist firmament. Soon he had become one of the Congress secretaries. Then he was elevated to the General Secretariat, a key post, to which he was reappointed year after year. It was almost a permanent job, but unlike most permanent jobs, it carried no salary.

After he had given his full time to this position for a number of years, Congress finally decided to pay him a modest salary. He would not have objected, having no other source of income, but when his father heard of it he became furious.

"I would lower my head in shame," he told his son, "if you accepted Congress money. You don't take money for services in a cause like this. Don't you have all you need in my house? Your family is well taken care of."

"That's all to the good, Father. But it's no pleasure to be financially dependent upon you."

Motilal finally won the argument. Though he, too, devoted much time to Congress work, he kept up his legal practice. It brought in enough funds to maintain the Nehru household in its present modest status.

So Jawaharlal remained a retainer in his father's house till Motilal's death in 1931. The son was now so absorbed in his task that financial problems did not matter much to him anymore.

The years of hectic political activity continued to be years of inner conflict. To the outside world Nehru appeared as a self-assured hero who knew exactly what he was fighting for, but in moments of reflection he was assailed by doubts.

Particularly painful were his doubts about his beloved spiritual master. Though at all times Gandhi's loyal and disciplined follower, he was never a yes-man. More than once he was on the point of breaking with the Mahatma. At such times he actually preferred to be shut away in prison, removed temporarily from painful decisions.

Once Gandhi called off a civil disobedience campaign that was in full swing when a group of peasants in a remote region stormed a police station and burned the building with everybody inside. "My brothers have disgraced the cause of *satyagraha,*" said the Mahatma. "India is not yet ready for it."

Jawaharlal was dumfounded. "Should anyone who got out of hand be able to halt our great fight?" he argued. "What if the other side planted agents to stir up violence?"

Another time Gandhi held a number of talks with the viceroy, Lord Irwin. Again he ordered all civil disobedience action stopped. He had come to an agreement with the Englishman and he wanted to signify his trust in him. But in reality the viceroy had only made vague promises with several crucial reservations. Jawaharlal went along with the Mahatma's commitments, but only, as he expressed it, "after great mental conflict."

Again and again the two clashed on the role of religion in the independence movement. For Gandhi it was mainly a giant spiritual revival, and when Nehru put forward his agnostic point of view, the Mahatma refused to believe him: "While Jawaharlal says he does not believe in God, he is nearer God than many who profess to be His worshippers." Jawaharlal's God, however, was not a personal deity; it was service to humanity and adherence to noble ethical standards.

There were other disturbing thoughts in Nehru's mind. He came to have strong misgivings about the Congress movement's narrow nationalistic goals. After a trip to Europe in 1925 which lasted almost two years, he was filled with the staggering problems of the world as a whole. He had left India with his wife and their eight-year-old daughter mainly because of Kamala's poor health, but he also longed to gain new perspectives.

They stayed mostly in Swiss mountain resorts, but Jawaharlal took side trips from there whenever possible. He observed the League of Nations at work and met many of its representatives. He saw social unrest in England where the coal miners were battling for better living conditions. In London he met an Indian youth with sharp aquiline features who dabbled in economics and in left-wing politics. His name was V. K. Krishna Menon. His keen intellect and razor-sharp sarcastic wit impressed Jawaharlal immediately, and the two have remained intimate friends ever since. Krishna Menon stayed in London for many years manning this very important listening post for the Congress organization and serving as its chief lobbyist and propagandist.

On a visit to Brussels Nehru joined the "League against Imperialism," made up of representatives from many colonial regions in Asia and Africa. Meeting those dark-skinned revolutionaries, he gained much insight into the problems of suppressed peoples. India was not alone in her quest for independence.

He also had a quick glance at Soviet Russia. In those days the U.S.S.R. interested, even fascinated, many intellectuals. Unaware of the oppressive cruelty with which the Communist regime operated, they had visions of a noble experiment in raising the Russian masses to a new level of freedom and happiness.

Jawaharlal returned to India, more convinced than ever of the need for sweeping social reforms. "Two things are dear to me," he declared in a speech, "independence for this country of ours and equality between man and man."

He persuaded Congress to begin social planning for the days of freedom ahead. Key industries should be nationalized, the power of the landlords curbed, free education, public housing and social welfare measures introduced. Such programs, often called socialistic, were already well established in many enlightened parts of the world. This stand for social progress made Jawaharlal the darling of the younger set in Congress.

Nehru's socialism has never wavered from its democratic and humanitarian base. He was repelled by the rigid dogmatism of Karl Marx and of the Communists, who allowed no free discussion, only blind acceptance. As for aping the Soviet methods in India, "It was absurd," he declared, "to copy blindly what had taken place in Russia."

But that was exactly what the small but noisy group of Indian Communists proposed. Nehru became the target of their most vicious attacks. "Instead of trying to convert people's minds," he observed, "they have largely concentrated on abuse of others."

He castigated the Reds of India and other countries for their slavelike submission to the commands of the Kremlin. Their policies, he realized, "could only be understood on the basis that what may be good for Russia must necessarily be good for the rest of the world."

So Congress moved along its own charted course, a respectable party one day and a secret underground organization the next. At times the whole movement was declared illegal and its officers jailed under many pretexts.

It was in those days that the women took over and continued the task of peaceful resistance. They were named as stand-bys for important positions and carried on for the men who were in prison.

At the height of the civil disobedience campaigns huge parades of women moved through the streets shouting slogans and singing nationalistic songs. Swarup and Krishna had their share of arrests, and, in the meantime, Indira formed a "monkey brigade" of children that carried Congress messages past British soldiers and police.

The great surprise of all who knew her was the appearance of Kamala on the public scene. This frail woman who spent most of her adult life under the curse of creeping illness threw herself into the freedom movement with all the strength she could muster. It was as if she wanted to prove to the world and to herself that she was more than a shadow cast by the brilliance of her husband.

Acutely sensitive, she must have felt strongly about her frailty, which prevented her from keeping up with Jawaharlal's grueling schedule. So she carved out a field of activity all of her own. Because she had suffered so much from the feeling of uselessness, she became an ardent advocate of women's emancipation.

With astonishment, people watched this member of a renowned Brahmin family talk to lowly women in the streets and in the market place, exhorting them to take a stand, to make their strength felt.

Though she had little formal education, she gained quite a reputation around Allahabad as a public speaker. With the male leaders away in prison, Kamala practically took charge of Congress activities in her home city, arranging meetings and boycotts, carrying on correspondence, drawing up resolutions.

A police cordon drawn across the thoroughfare once halted a demonstration which she was leading. In silent protest the women squatted down on the pavement before the policemen. It was a much-practiced Gandhian technique, a contest in patience and endurance. An acquaintance who knew of Kamala's delicate health brought her a blanket. Hours later the same friend came back to the spot. The demonstrators were still facing the police lines. In the chill of the evening Kamala was shivering under her flimsy sari, while an old woman, not far away, sat snuggly wrapped in the blanket.

During one of his prison sentences, Jawaharlal learned about an incident that made his blood boil. His mother had marched in a political parade which was stopped by the police. The *lathees* went into action. The elderly woman was repeatedly hit and knocked down. For some time she lay by the roadside, bleeding and unconscious. Finally a police officer who recognized her put her into his car and brought her home. Several weeks later, when she came to visit her son in jail, her head was still bandaged. She shrugged the whole thing off. "It was a privilege," she said, "to share those hardships with the younger volunteers."

After visiting hours, Jawaharlal was alone with his thoughts. "I wonder," he mused, "how I would have behaved if I had been there. How far would my nonviolence have carried me? Not very far, I fear, for that sight would have made me forget the long lesson I had tried to learn for more than a dozen years."

In between jail terms, when Jawaharlal submerged himself in the mainstream of hectic political activity, Gandhi came to rely more and more upon the younger man's assistance. As the years went by it became evident that Nehru was being groomed for the successorship to the Mahatma's purple. "Gandhi's Crown Prince," they called him jokingly. That Jawaharlal stood on many issues far to the left of his *guru* did not bother the aging Gandhi. "He is undoubtedly an extremist," was his opinion, "thinking far ahead of his surroundings. But he is humble enough not to force the pace to the breaking point. He is pure as crystal, he is truthful beyond suspicion."

Barely forty years old, Jawaharlal was elected to the presidency of the National Congress in 1929. He was to hold this post many more times. But this was a unique occasion, for his predecessor who now handed him the president's gavel was none other than his own father.

The city of Lahore, where this memorable meeting was held, broke out in a triumphant celebration. Through the aisles of the tent city that had been erected for the visitors rode the president-elect on a white charger. Members of the Congress Youth League surrounded their idol, and behind them trotted a herd of elephants.

Jawaharlal Nehru was on his way.

9.

TOWARD SWARAJ

JAWAHARLAL NEHRU was on his way—to prison.

Part of his first presidential year was spent in Naini Central Prison, the correctional institution of Allahabad. While Motilal once more took up the gavel to substitute for his son, Jawaharlal lived in complete isolation. Over two thousand prisoners were all around him, only yards away, but he was considered too dangerous to meet them. His universe was an enclosure formed by a wall fifteen feet high.

Lying on a bed that was chained to the wall, he listened to the prison noises during the endless nights, and they seemed to come from wild animals in the forest.

For the roaming eyes there was nothing to look at but the circular walls surrounding his little shed, nicknamed the "doghouse." Once it had been used to keep violent criminals away from the others. The round walls oppressed Jawaharlal to the point where he imagined himself on the bottom of a deep well. I wonder if, he thought, or is it a fact that, a circular wall reminds me more of captivity than a rectangular one? The absence of corners and edges adds to the sense of oppression.

After some time, he was permitted to leave the enclosure and walk for half an hour in the large prison yard. But this occurred only in the early dawn when the other convicts were not yet about. During this precious half-hour, instead of walking, Nehru ran. He managed to cover over two miles every day to the amazement of the guards, who thought he had already lost his mind.

Motilal Nehru served as acting Congress president for two and a half months, then he himself was arrested. Jawaharlal's solitary confinement came to an end, as his father and two other prominent nationalists joined him in his cell.

Jawaharlal tried to adhere to a strict daily routine. After his vigorous exercise period at four in the morning, he did household chores, such as cleaning the shed and washing his clothes and his father's. In traditional Hindu fashion the son waited on the father, who was now well along in years and not in the best of health. Reading and discussion took up the remainder of the day. But there was also a period of about three hours devoted to spinning on an old-fashioned wheel. Gandhi's shadow penetrated the thickest prison walls.

In his double capacity as prisoner and prominent public figure, Jawaharlal ran into some unusual situations. Inmates of penitentiaries are not, as a rule, taken by official conveyance so that they can hold conferences with inmates of other such institutions. But that is exactly what happened. It was a critical moment in the political tug-of-war. The British government had made new suggestions for the ending of civil disobedience. To ponder these suggestions the three leading nationalists had to be brought together. They were all in jail.

On direct orders from the viceroy, the two Nehrus were put on a special train and, under heavy guard, dispatched to Poona Jail where Gandhi was lodged. They traveled only at night, halting at forlorn wayside stations to take on coal and supplies. Despite all secrecy, large crowds of peasants greeted them with garlands of flowers at every stop. Nobody could figure out how the news had spread. The crowds were even larger when the train sped back after the three-day conference. India's spokesmen were returned to their cells, and civil disobedience continued.

Kamala's poor health was a constant worry to her imprisoned husband. With a mixture of pride and anxiety he received the news of her growing public activities. For some time the government hesitated to imprison women, but the female Congress volunteers courted arrest. They practically demanded to share the fate of their menfolk. Jail became the mark of equality. Finally they had their wish.

On New Year's Day of 1931 Kamala was taken to prison. Since women in paddywagons were still somewhat of a novelty, the newspapers wrote long accounts about it, and Jawaharlal read them all in his cell. As Kamala was led away, a reporter asked her for a statement. "I am happy beyond measure and proud to follow in the footsteps of my husband," she replied. "I hope the people will keep the flag flying."

Jawaharlal tried to picture the new Kamala in her heroic role. Yet he could not suppress a smile. Those high-sounding words suggested that all she wanted was to tag along behind her husband. "Probably she would not have said just that," he decided, "if she had thought over the matter, for she considered herself a champion of women's rights against the tyranny of men."

Proud Kamala: anxious to be a partner to her spouse, not just a glorified servant as Hindu tradition demanded.

Indian freedom was not won in a day. The struggle lasted for over a quarter of a century, punctuated by successes and defeats and long periods of stagnation.

During most of those years Jawaharlal held top positions in the movement, positions that gratified his burning ambition and flattered his considerable vanity. But not for one single moment did he deny that Mohandas Gandhi remained the undisputed final authority. Even when the shriveled old man in the loincloth held no Congress office, his consent was absolutely essential for all important actions. He constantly sharpened and refined the weapons in the arsenal of civil disobedience.

In 1930 the Mahatma decided to defy the government's monopoly on the sale of salt. From his home he began a march of 250 miles toward the sea. As he proceeded, day after day, thousands of followers fell in behind him. Staff in hand, he strode at the head of the huge procession like a second Moses. He was then sixty-one years old.

By the time he reached the seashore the march had attracted world-wide attention. He dipped an earthen pail into the salt water, and when the water had evaporated there was, on the bottom, a misshapen little clump of salt.

At first, Nehru had not been at all enthusiastic about the Mahatma's most recent brain child. It was a primitive gesture and, of course, completely outmoded. Gandhi's excursions into the past always irritated the scientific-minded Jawaharlal. But he had to admit, once again, that his leader had shown the most ingenious insight into the people's mind. The salt march was something every peasant understood, for even the poorest villager had to buy salt from the government.

Again a law had intentionally been broken.

Then came the no-tax campaign. This was a very painful step, not only for the collectors of revenue, but even more for those who refused to pay taxes and rents. In retaliation, the authorities seized property and levied fines, and more property was confiscated when the fines remained unpaid.

In the Nehru household, the finance officers, accompanied by a detachment of police, became frequent visitors. They seized cars, jewelry and furniture in default of taxes. Jawaharlal had to quiet his remaining servants, who wanted to resist the police by force.

The government's final answer to the defiance of the tax laws was again the penitentiary. The jail cell became the coveted place of honor for the Congress volunteers. When mass arrests were made, hundreds of young enthusiasts stormed the police vans clamoring not to be left out. At court the accused never defended themselves and cheerfully accepted their sentences.

Once inside the prison gates, this new type of inmate was a gigantic headache for their keepers. They were so vastly different from the wretches usually in their charge. Not only were they educated, but they were fearless, insisting on their rights and talking back to their jailers. But they were also cooperative and held no personal grudge.

Once again the Nehrus, father and son, were locked up together with a number of their co-workers. The prison was badly overcrowded, and the superintendent would have been happy to see a number of the newcomers escape. "Look the other way and let some of them climb over the wall or rush out when you bring their mail," he told the turnkey who had charge of the political prisoners. "No harm will befall you. On the contrary, if you get rid of them, I'll recommend you for a promotion."

It sounded very attractive, but the poor jailer never had a chance to earn his promotion. The "politicals" stayed till their hour of release.

All this behavior, opposition without physical attack, suffering without resistance, was incomprehensible to the British. Behind every move they suspected a sinister conspiracy. Yet it was all in the open. "All our cards are on the table," insisted Nehru.

The marriage of his sister Swarup caused a minor panic in Allahabad. Since both Nehrus were then prominent Congress leaders, hundreds of friends and followers streamed into the city for the wedding. In fact, they combined this celebration with one of their regular annual sessions, since practically all important Congress workers were on hand. However, the Englishmen living in the city became extremely worried. They armed themselves with revolvers and kept close watch on their native servants, suspicious that they might be secretly plotting with the visitors.

Of course, nothing happened. There was just a peaceful meeting and a traditional wedding.

Swarup married Ranjit S. Pandit, a scholarly historian, who was to die in prison in 1944. Following an old custom she changed both her family name and her given name and became Vijaya Lakshmi Pandit. She is now known all over the world as Madame Pandit, the first Indian woman to hold the post of provincial minister. Later, as an ambassador and president of the United Nations General Assembly, she moved into the ranks of the most renowned women of our time.

While the English often displayed the cruelty and haughtiness of the slavemaster toward the Gandhians, they were also capable of a humanitarian and chivalrous spirit not found among any other conquering nations. Over the dull thuds of police clubs and the shots from military rifles could often be heard enlightened voices from the island nation that had pioneered fairness in courts, social welfare and many philanthropic causes. Some students of India have tried to speculate how Gandhi would have fared with his techniques if his adversaries had been not the British, but, let us say, Hitler or Stalin.

Even behind prison walls a certain code of chivalry governed, at times, the relations between jailer and jailed. Jawaharlal seldom felt any bitterness against individuals and gratefully acknowledged any personal kindness shown him.

Once when he was about to be transferred to another jail, the superintendent approached him somewhat shamefacedly and pressed a package into his hand. "This is a bundle of old German magazines," he said. "I heard you were trying to study German."

Nehru was very thankful for such little gestures. But more deeply he appreciated the privileges of repeated temporary release from confinement when illness and tragedy struck

within the family circle. Then the wall of distrust between
Indian and Britisher disappeared for a time. "To each,"
Nehru once wrote, "the other appeared as a sour-looking,
unamiable creature, and neither realized that there was
decency and kindliness behind the mask."

When the Nehrus shared a cell again, Jawaharlal observed
his father wasting away by his side, unable to do anything
more for him than relieve him of some prison chores. Motilal's condition became very grave. He was released from
jail when the shadow of death was already upon him, despite
his own protests against such favorable treatment. Then
Jawaharlal too was released before his time was up, so that
he could attend to his dying father. He was with him when
the end came.

The funeral of Motilal Nehru turned into a national day
of mourning. Untold thousands followed the body as it was
carried to the cremation platform.

But as the pace of the civil disobedience campaigns quickened, England became increasingly alarmed. The British
political parties differed sharply in their attitudes toward the
movement. While the Conservatives were for the traditional
"get tough" methods, Liberals and Laborites wanted to come
to terms with the new India. Eventually everybody, with the
exception of a few die-hards, began to realize that self-government was only a matter of time.

In 1935 the Government of India Act was issued, which
British statesmen considered a very generous concession.
Though ultimate authority remained with the viceroy, the
law gave the colony a federal structure and a larger measure
of self-rule. Over thirty million Indians received the right
to vote. In large numbers, Hindus and Moslems entered the
sumptuous government buildings, formerly strictly taboo to
them, and became provincial ministers and legislators.

Congress turned into an official political party with its own
list of candidates, and Jawaharlal Nehru became its most
successful campaigner. More than ten million people lis-

tened to his speeches. In seven out of the eleven provincial legislatures the Congress delegates obtained majorities.

Still the nationalist government marched on. There was no stopping it till the final goal, complete independence, was reached. And Jawaharlal continued to shuttle back and forth between freedom and confinement, between hectic activity and enforced idleness. It was like an interminable jumping from scalding hot to ice-cold showers and back again.

10.

PRIVATE LIFE OF A PEACEFUL REBEL

JAWAHARLAL AND KAMALA were driving home in their car from a meeting of peasants in a nearby village. Their mood was buoyant. The shouts of admiration, the simple applause of simple people, were still ringing in their ears. It was a warm fragrant night filled with the soft noises of the Indian plains.

The automobile had just left the rural dirt road and entered the paved street in the outskirts of the city. Suddenly the shrill whine of a police whistle broke the magic spell of the summer night. A clipped voice shouted an order, and the car ground to a stop at the curb. Uniformed men surrounded it.

There was no need to ask the meaning of all this. Kamala, her slender body suddenly shivering under the silk stole, clung to her husband.

"Only eight days since you came home from prison." Her voice was husky, but she did not cry.

"Eight days of freedom," sighed Jawaharlal as he stroked her forehead. "They seemed like one day, no more."

He turned to the arresting officer, "I am ready, sir."

A "Black Maria" took him away into the night.

The arrests came at all hours, but mostly at night to avoid rousing his followers in the streets. Jawaharlal was whisked away from his home, from his office, from railroad stations. Once a train in which he was riding was halted in the middle of nowhere. A police van was parked beside the tracks, and soon he was again on his way to free lodgings, courtesy of the British government.

Altogether Jawaharlal Nehru spent 3,262 days behind bars, a rather unique and painful training period for the post of India's chief executive. He was confined to jail on nine different occasions, the shortest visit lasting twelve days, the longest almost three years.

No matter what the reason or the circumstances, this forced removal from the normal pattern of life for such a long time was bound to have a strong impact on the mind. Nehru's character can only be properly understood in the light of this drawn-out ordeal.

At times, imprisonment was comparatively mild. The political prisoners could roam the length and width of the compound. They even organized classes in reading and writing for the other inmates, most of whom were illiterates. Visitors came frequently, and there was no dearth of books and newspapers.

The contact with the ordinary convict gave Jawaharlal quite a shock. The whole prison system was riddled with corruption. An incompetent and ridiculously underpaid staff saw its main function in the extorting of money from the prisoners and their relatives for better food and other little comforts. The prison fare was wretched beyond comparison. Inmates were treated with callous indifference and premeditated brutality. Not the slightest attempt was made to reform them.

Breaches of rules were commonly punished by flogging. Jawaharlal witnessed the "disciplining" of a sixteen-year-old boy, arrested for a political offense. He was stripped and tied to the whipping triangle. As each stripe fell on him and cut into his flesh, he shouted, "Victory to Mahatma Gandhi," till he fainted.

Nehru discovered that charity and basic goodness could be found among the men inside the gray walls perhaps more often than on the outside. Once a blind prisoner was being discharged after thirteen years. He was leaving empty-handed, without hope for support or understanding. His fellow convicts collected their pitiful possessions and deposited them for him at the prison office. One gave his only shirt. Another had just shown Jawaharlal with pride a new pair of sandals. He parted with them so that their blind comrade would not have to begin his new life barefoot.

Many of the prisoners were "lifers," vegetating day after day through a senseless, machinelike existence. A lifer who had heard why Nehru was in prison came up to him. "I know what you're fighting for," he whispered. "What of us lifers? Will independence take us out of this hell?"

This was a problem the planners of the new India had not thought of yet.

Prisons differed greatly from one another. In some, there was the utter misery of prolonged solitary confinement, whereas in others privacy was completely lacking.

One sentence was served in a barracks where about fifty men were crowded together, day and night. Bathing, household chores, the most discreet functions, had to be carried out in public. "It was the dull side of family life," Jawaharlal observed, "magnified a hundredfold, with few of its graces and compensations, and all this among people of all kinds and tastes."

When he could, he stole away in the early morning hours to lie in the open enclosure in front of the barracks. There he would await the sunrise. He watched the ever-shifting monsoon clouds in the paling sky. The shades of blue and gray up there contrasted joyously with the eternal drabness of the mud-colored barracks walls. The prisoner's vivid imagination magnified the clouds into fantastic shapes tinted in riotous hues.

When shut away in a lonely cell, Jawaharlal took up some of the ancient yoga exercises. His favorite was a slow, sustained headstand, because "the slightly comic position increased my good humor and made me a little more tolerant of life's vagaries." The topsy-turvy world around him seemed less so when viewed upside down.

Jawaharlal was bent on finding outlets for his emotions, stunted and puny though they had to remain. He had always been a lover of nature, and it was torture to be shut off from things that grow in the great outdoors.

One of his many cells, located in a large city, was about ten feet by nine. Two chimneys, right in front of the prison yard, belched continuous clouds of black smoke. When he craned his neck he could barely make out the tops of two trees in an adjoining yard. Their branches were bare. Still they were alive. Gradually he saw them break out with buds, and the dismal panorama appeared almost cheerful.

However dreary the surroundings, there was always a piece of sky above. Jawaharlal requested astronomical books and charts. He learned to recognize the stars and planets, and knowing their orbits, he awaited their appearance as if they were old acquaintances.

What prisoners long to hear most is the sound of women's voices and of children's laughter. Nehru tried to find meager substitutes in the noises of such animals as ventured into his secluded world. For a time a sick puppy, abandoned by one of the guards, became his companion. He brought it back to health, spending many a night at this nursing task. With fascination he watched the lizards that rushed across the hard earth floor and the sparrows that built their nests in the holes of the roof.

One day he observed a fierce fight between two male parrots with green feathers and red bills. He was amused to see the female, for whose favor they were slashing at each other, sitting calmly by, unruffled and cool, awaiting the outcome of the battle.

Squirrels came to visit his cell. When he sat motionless with a book in his hand, they often clambered trustfully up his leg and rested for a moment on his knee, peering at him with inquisitive eyes.

"I realized," he wrote, "that while I complained of loneliness, that little yard, which seemed empty and deserted, was teeming with life. All of these creeping or crawling insects lived their lives without interfering with me in any way, and I saw no reason why I should interfere with them." But his nonviolence did not extend to bedbugs and mosquitoes, and he had a horror of bats that flew soundlessly out of the dusk and passed within an inch of his face.

Whenever he could Jawaharlal took to gardening. With infinite care he tended a bit of lawn in the corner of the wall or nurtured a tiny vegetable patch. He and other political prisoners once drew water for their plants from an old well by walking around and around the well, yoked together in pairs, as the bullocks are made to do on the farm.

Prison was Nehru's graduate and postgraduate university. As in his lonely youth, books were the substitutes for live companions. Travel books, maps, atlases, were among his favorites. Hemmed in by those cruel walls, his spirit went on safaris to the most romantic places on earth.

He also kept up a program of massive reading in philosophy, political science, economics and history. And he was, of course, most anxious to keep abreast of current affairs at home and abroad. For prolongued periods Jawaharlal was out of touch with developments in his own movement, and he was forced to be an observer rather than an active participant. His viewpoint became detached and critical. Soul-searching and self-examination have remained life habits of his ever since.

"Whenever I come to your cell," remarked one puzzled jail superintendent, "I find you reading. It almost gets on my nerves. As far as I'm concerned, I had finished all my reading at the age of twelve." Which did not prevent this model British civil servant from obtaining, in due time, the rank of colonel and the position of Inspector-General of Prisons. When he came to inspect, a huge state umbrella was held over him, and the prisoners had to bow deeply and shout, "*Salaam*." But no books for him.

It was in jail that Jawaharlal Nehru wrote several books of his own that put him in the forefront of contemporary authors. He proved himself a born writer, as well as a born statesman. But the statesman in him might never have given the writer an opportunity had it not been for those countless vacant hours of confinement. Bending over his manuscripts in various cheerless cells, he could not help recalling how great writers of the past, such as Cervantes who created the immortal *Don Quixote* and John Bunyan who wrote the *Pilgrim's Progress,* had to do their work under similar conditions.

The first book, *Glimpses of World History*, grew from a collection of letters to his daughter Indira. It was begun in the comfort of the family home in Allahabad and concluded during a prison term in 1933.

Indira's education was a cause of great concern to her parents. Normally she would have been sent to an English school, but that was out now on account of the boycott of all things British. With some misgivings she was kept home under the guidance of tutors. Later she was sent to a college founded by the famous Indian poet and nationalist Rabindranath Tagore.

Even while living at home, Indira saw very little of her father, who was either busy with his political work or in jail. Fearing that her budding mind was not receiving enough stimulation, Nehru decided to carry on a kind of informal correspondence course with his daughter. He wrote the first letter in the broiling summer heat of 1928 when he was kept busy in the city while the girl had been sent to the cool mountains:

When you and I are together, you often ask me questions about many things, and I try to answer them. Now that you are at Mussoorie and I am in Allahabad we cannot have these talks. I am therefore going to write to you from time to time short accounts of the story of our earth and the many countries, great and small, into which it is divided.

The letters sketch the geological past of our planet, then describe prehistoric man and finally turn to world history. Written in simple language, the book gives proper credit to both Eastern and Western thoughts and deeds. It is a remarkable piece of writing, especially when one considers that Nehru is neither a professional geologist nor a historian and that most of it was composed in jail without the benefit of any reference material.

During the short intervals between prison terms, Jawaharlal now had to attend to his duties as the head of the family. On one such occasion he saw to the arrangements for the wedding of his younger sister Krishna, who had only recently herself been discharged from jail. Due to those circumstances and because their mother was also ill at that time, the wedding was a simple civil ceremony, quite a contrast to Jawaharlal's own glittering nuptials many years earlier.

He could not escape the money problems which had always annoyed him. On one of his holidays at home, he surveyed the family's financial situation and found it disastrous. The bills had been piling up, and now the creditors were becoming impatient. There were no more saddle horses and lush carpets to sell.

As he sat at his desk brooding over a sheet that was covered with figures, an arm draped itself over his shoulders. The slight caress could barely be felt. Kamala stood behind him holding a small box, a fine piece of handiwork in sandalwood with inlaid mother-of-pearl.

Her husband turned in his chair. "Why, this is your jewelry box. What do you want with it so early in the morning? Are you planning to attend a feast?"

"Take it and sell what's in it."

He was taken aback. Finances had not been discussed between them lately, but she had guessed.

"No, I won't have it. I'll raise the money somehow."

"Take it, Jawahar. I haven't worn any of these for ages. Diamonds and rubies don't go very well with *khadi*."

He had to admit that she was right. Glittering pins and necklaces were out of place on the homespun garments of Gandhi's peaceful army. Soon the precious stones were locked up in the strongbox of a merchant, somewhere in a dark cavern of the bazaar section.

Nothing more had been said about it, but the two felt closer to each other than they ever had before.

She was more beautiful now than on her wedding day, still slender as a young willow. Her dainty limbs moved gracefully. Childlike gaiety often lit up her small face. On the rare occasions when they traveled as a family, people sometimes took her and Indira to be sisters. Balding Jawaharlal with his gray fringe of hair and the creases in his high forehead was uncertain whether he should feel proud or hurt.

The political turmoil left them hardly any opportunity for the usual privacy of married life. The last family vacation they were able to take was a delightful experience. With their daughter they visited the island of Ceylon, the nearest spot away from the commotion of Indian public affairs.

They took a little house, just the three of them. But even there they faced a constant coming and going of well-wishers from all classes, often walking many miles to see them and to bring simple gifts: flowers, vegetables, homemade butter. The house overflowed with the presents, and they were passed on to hospitals and orphanages.

The Nehrus drove about to visit the lush tropical forests and the tea plantations. They stood in the courtyards of ancient monasteries and gazed at the countless statues of Buddha, the gentle teacher of the Middle Path.

Returning to India, they swung leisurely through several

princely states in the southern part of the peninsula, visiting friends and sight-seeing like ordinary tourists.

In one city, still strongly tradition-bound, a group of women gathered at a reception in honor of Kamala. They were not yet conditioned to mixed social affairs for both sexes. Soon Kamala, in her straightforward way, was lecturing her hostesses on the new struggle of women against male domination. She must have made a deep impression, for, some time later, she received a letter from the husband of one of the ladies. "Ever since hearing you talk," the poor man complained, "my wife has been impossible to live with. Once docile and obedient, as a woman ought to be, she now ignores my wishes and talks back when I reprimand her. She argues continuously. . . ."

They were in Calcutta when Jawaharlal was presented with his next warrant of arrest. Kamala went to their hotel room to collect his clothes. He followed her to say good-by. For a moment she clung to him and then collapsed in a faint. Except for a few short moments during visiting hours in prison, he was never to see her on her feet again.

With increasing speed the dread pulmonary tuberculosis was draining all reserves of strength from her body. It did not help matters that she refused to follow doctor's orders for rest but carried on her political work till she was ready to collapse.

In his utter helplessness, Jawaharlal suffered agonies of depression. He felt certain that his being away in prison had something to do with Kamala's weakening. If he could only be at her side, things would be different.

To keep his mental balance he reached again for the pen. He was not thinking, at the time, of publication, just of a device to straighten out the tangle of thoughts that tumbled through his mind. This exercise in mental self-help resulted in the remarkable autobiography, *Toward Freedom*. Except for a postscript it was written entirely in prison.

In its pages a human soul reveals itself without any reservation. Many famous people have written their memoirs with the obvious intention of glorifying their accomplishments and finding excuses for their mistakes. Not so Nehru. With brutal frankness he analyzes his actions and the motives behind them. He probes into the innermost recesses of his mind. Nobody, it seems, is a sharper critic of Nehru than Nehru himself.

The book contains the musings of a lonely soul. Most of it, he admits, was "written under peculiarly distressing circumstances when I was suffering from depression and emotional strain. Perhaps some of this is reflected in what I have written, but this very writing helped me greatly to pull myself out of the present with all its worries."

In the summer of 1934 he was writing the final chapters. It was a sultry night. The turnkey opened the door and then stood respectfully aside to let the superintendent himself enter.

"Wash up, Mr. Nehru, and change your clothes. You're leaving in half an hour."

"Where to? Why?"

"You'll be taken to Allahabad. Orders from the highest quarters."

That was all he would say.

A car with three silent police officers carried him through the night. It rumbled along the rutted road, bumping into the plowed fields to avoid hitting the placidly ruminating sacred cows.

At the police station of his home town Jawaharlal was given an explanation. Kamala's illness had become critical. He was being temporarily released to be with her, another gesture of kindliness on the part of the British masters.

Doctors and nurses were rushing about when Nehru entered his home. On the white pillow Kamala's face looked unbelievably small. Hour after hour he sat by her side, feeling her burning forehead, holding her dry hand. He talked to her, and she answered when she could, or she just smiled, happy that he was there. Mostly she was too exhausted to answer his anxious questions.

Nehru found out how painful it was, at times, to be a public figure. Again and again he was called away from the sickroom. Party officials came to brief him, to ask for his opinion, his support.

The whole independence movement was in a slump. The volunteers were disheartened. The struggle had lasted so long, and still the end was not in sight. Personal squabbles marred the scene, and resentment between Hindus and Moslems became noticeable. The advocates of a do-nothing policy seemed to dominate Congress at the moment.

Nehru felt like shouting at his old comrades, "Come, pull out of it. Don't lose sight of our great goal."

But he remained silent. His heart was with the patient in the sickroom, and, besides, he felt honor-bound to refrain from politics. The courtesy shown him by the government merited such behavior. Though he had given no formal promise, it was the response expected from a gentleman.

How long would he be allowed to stay? He was legally still a prisoner. Every noise made him turn nervously toward the door. Was it the knock of the policeman come to take him back?

A day passed, and then another. A whole week had gone by, and the knock on the door had not yet sounded.

Later he was to find out that the question of his rearrest had been heatedly debated on the highest governmental level. There was political pressure and counterpressure, both in India and in England. The viceroy himself became involved, and so did cabinet ministers and members of Parliament.

To take him back into custody would be branded around the world as one more act of imperialistic callousness. But to leave Nehru free was too dangerous. Congress was to convene shortly, and elections under the new Government of India Act were coming up. Officialdom would breathe a lot easier if he were not around to do mischief during the campaign.

Kamala's doctors had to file daily bulletins about her health, which were carefully examined in various bureaus. The authorities were anxiously waiting for the crisis to pass.

Jawaharlal had almost settled back into the habits of free men when the dreaded knock at the door finally came. The officer presenting the warrant fidgeted in acute embarrassment. A fleeting kiss on the forehead of his sleeping wife, and then Jawaharlal tiptoed out of the room. As he was stepping into the police car, his mother, also ailing and getting feebler by the day, ran up to him with arms outstretched, tears running down her wrinkled face. She had always before managed to compose herself. Her features kept haunting him for many a long night.

Freedom had lasted exactly eleven days.

Prison life now became unmitigated torture. The days crept by with intolerable slowness as he waited for news from home. His only relief was the work on the autobiography, which, in many places, bears the mark of those trying days.

For a while he received daily reports from the doctors, passed on to him in a complicated procedure through the Allahabad police and the prison office. Then they stopped.

He was given to understand that the powers-that-be would be only too glad to release him permanently. All that was needed was a little promise—an informal assurance would suffice—to keep quiet on political matters.

His conscience wrestled with the alternatives. Kamala needed him by her side; there was no doubt about it. Perhaps his presence might make the difference between life and death. But such a promise would violate all the ground rules of civil disobedience. It would make him a traitor to his political creed, though politics was, at the moment, far from his mind.

But was it really moral conviction that kept him from giving such an assurance? Or was it just personal pride and fear for his political future?

For about six weeks this dilemma assailed his mind. Then came another visit home, sudden and unexplained. This time he was only allowed to stay for a few hours. Kamala was lying in a daze, raked by high fever, but as he was leaving she smiled and motioned for him to bend down. "What is this," she whispered, "about your giving an assurance to the government? Don't give it."

That closed the matter.

It had long been decided that Kamala needed a change of climate. As soon as she felt a little better, she was to go to a mountain resort. But she was getting worse instead of better. The physicians could see no gain in waiting any longer. The day before she was to leave for Bhowali in the Himalayan foothills, Jawaharlal was taken to bid her good-by.

The next time he saw her was three weeks later, on his way to a new jail. In another magnanimous gesture the authorities had him transferred to a prison in the mountains where he could be nearer to his wife. Had it not been for the tragic circumstances, he could almost have enjoyed his new domicile with snow-capped peaks as constant company and the hillside afire with peach and plum blossoms.

He was allowed to leave his mountain prison for several short visits. Each time the bond between husband and wife seemed stronger, the farewell more painful.

Kamala's frail body failed to respond to any treatment. As a last resort, she was taken to Europe. For Jawaharlal there were no more visits, only interminable days and nights that stretched into months.

In the autumn of 1935 the reports from the sanitarium in Germany's Black Forest became alarming.

Suddenly he was released, five and a half months before his sentence was up. When a prisoner leaves the place of his confinement, he stops at the gate to stretch his limbs, to drink in the delicious air of freedom, to treat his starved eyes to the sight of color and movement. But Nehru had no time for this. He rushed home to pack and was off to the airport. Five days after leaving jail he was in the town of Badenweiler with Kamala.

She greeted him with quiet joy. Her thin face radiated new hope as he sat by her.

Life settled into a new pattern. Twice a day he trudged from the little *pension* where he was staying to the sanitarium. They would talk awhile, never very long, for she was too weak for sustained conversation. Kamala spoke of the future. She believed in it. There was so much she still wanted to do.

When her head sank back into the pillows and her eyes closed from exhaustion, he sat silently by her side. Sometimes he read to her from new books, a few pages at a time.

In the long evenings he walked along the forest paths that were strewn with needles and cones. Once more he had lots of time on his hands for brooding.

When he looked over the gently rolling hills, he had to remind himself forcefully that he was in Germany. In this peaceful corner it was hard to realize that in cities not far away, the jackboots of Nazi storm troopers were stomping the pavement. Hitler was in power. His voice screeched hate and violence, seconded by Fascist dictator Mussolini and by the war lords of Japan. Clouds of impending catastrophe darkened the sky.

Alone in his room, Jawaharlal forced himself to put the finishing touches to the autobiography, revising and editing the manuscript he had brought along from India.

Winter came early. Now he had to plow his way through snow and slush. He longed to be in the warmer climes to which he was accustomed. Kamala too was tired of Badenweiler. The place depressed her, especially after the death of a fellow patient, a young Irishman who had visited her sometimes and sent her flowers.

In January they left the Black Forest. Stricken now also by angina pectoris, Kamala was taken to Lausanne, Switzerland. Both of them liked the change. Not only was the scenery beautiful, but they also breathed the air of a free country and were nearer their daughter, who was attending a Swiss school and came to see them often.

Jawaharlal chafed under the forced inactivity. Whenever Kamala felt a shade better, he slipped away, for a day or two, to Paris or London. In the British capital he renewed the acquaintance of Krishna Menon, who helped him find a publisher for *Toward Freedom*. The book became an instant success in many parts of the world, even in England, which was sharply castigated in many of its pages.

India, too, was calling, and the call was loud and strong. Emissaries came to see him, and mountains of letters piled up in his room.

For the second time Jawaharlal had been elected to the presidency of the Indian National Congress. Again and again he read the summons and turned it over in his mind during sleepless nights.

The presidency: that meant return to India for the general session in the spring. It was for the president to mastermind the complex strategy at what might turn out to be the most crucial moment in the long fight for independence.

What was he to do? Once more a painful dilemma confronted him. Could he leave Kamala now? Was it right to sit around, wasting the days away in uselessness?

He had to come to a decision: leave Europe or resign from the Congress presidency.

Just then Kamala appeared to show slight improvement. "You must go," she insisted. "After the Congress session is over you can come back to me."

So passage to India was booked. Indira came from her school to spend those last days with her parents.

Jawaharlal was uneasy. "I will not stay long," he assured Kamala, as well as himself. "In two or three months I'll be back. Perhaps even earlier. And if I am needed, a cable will bring me here in a matter of days."

He packed his bag. Then the doctor asked to see him. "Perhaps you could postpone your departure for a week or so."

He would not say more. New plane reservations were made. There was no strength left in Kamala's emaciated body. She seemed to have lost the will to live. Her mind wandered from the confines of reality. "Somebody's in the room with us," she breathed to her husband. "He is calling me."

The end came as the night made way for the first glimmer of dawn. In the crematorium of Lausanne her delicate body was reduced to an urnful of ashes.

Now there was nothing to hold Nehru in Europe. Stopping between planes in Rome, he was invited to an interview with Benito Mussolini, the dictator of Italy. A high Fascist official met him at the airport.

"The *Duce* will be glad to receive you at six o'clock this evening," he declared.

"This is very kind, but Signor Mussolini will have to excuse me. I'm in no mood for audiences."

The smartly uniformed Fascist paled. This had never happened before. When the *Duce* expressed a wish, one did not refuse. He guessed that the real reason for the Indian's hesitance was the fear that Mussolini would use the interview for propaganda purposes.

"The *Duce* only wants to express his condolences. There will be no pictures, no reporters."

But Nehru remained adamant. The Italian finally left him, shivering under his bemedaled black shirt at the thought of what Mussolini would do to him in his wrath.

A large crowd awaited Jawaharlal as he arrived in Allahabad. Leaving his luggage in the care of an assistant, he stepped into the street. In his hand he held a small basket, inside of which was an urn. Followed by his friends he carried it to the bank of the Ganges River, a short distance away, and scattered the ashes of his wife over the waters so that they might return to the endless ocean from which all life flowed.

Before plunging anew into the swirl of public activity, he cabled his publisher:

"Just decided on dedication for autobiography:

To Kamala Who Is No More."

11.

THE GOAL IS NEAR

THE CAMPAIGN FOR the general elections was in full swing.

Three cars were speeding through the night as fast as the rutted country road would permit. It was almost four in the morning, but the last meeting on the day's program was still to be held. Jawaharlal and his party had made their first stop of the day eighteen hours earlier. Since then he had covered over four hundred miles and spoken at half a dozen monster rallies. In addition, there had been several unscheduled stops in obscure villages where the peasants had stood body to body to greet their hero.

Jawaharlal was soundly asleep in the last car as the little caravan halted by the bend of a small river. The ghostly flicker of torches illuminated a stretch of sandy beach framed by a dark wall of trees. The open space was packed with human shadows, pressed together in tight masses or moving about on the outer edges of the crowd. They had been waiting since the early evening.

With an ear-splitting roar that drove frightened game deeper into the forest the peasants now closed ranks and pressed toward the wooden bridge where the cars had halted. Excited as children examining a new toy, they watched Nehru's companions string cables and mount several loud-speakers on trees. None of them had ever seen such weird things before.

Then Jawaharlal stood on the roof of a sedan, microphone in hand. His helpers had struggled desperately to shake him

113

awake, but now his eyes shone and his face was flushed, as the crowds enveloped him in the warm, intoxicating embrace of their admiration.

"Hail to Mother India," they shouted.

"What does this mean what you are calling?" he asked them in his schoolmasterly manner.

Silence. They did not know.

"Who is this mother you salute?"

Again silence. Then a hesitant voice: "It is the earth."

"Whose earth? Your village earth? Your province?"

They were confused. "Explain it to us, *Panditji,*" they asked.

He told them that this mother was all India and that they were all her children. "You are her sons and daughters, you and all our brothers and sisters throughout Hindustan."

Only after he had painfully explained to them the idea of nationhood did he turn to the subject of voting. He did not mention the names of the local candidates. He had not even bothered to remember them. He was campaigning for freedom, not just for a Mr. Singh or a Mr. Gopal.

"I promise you nothing," he told the listeners who shivered in their thin garments, "except unceasing struggle till freedom is attained. Vote for us only if you understand and accept our program and if you are prepared to live up to it. Otherwise we don't want your vote."

It was an unusual campaign speech, but it left the listeners in a spirit of awe and reverence. The cheers at the end of the meeting were much more subdued than they had been at the speaker's arrival.

The cars lurched away, leaving behind a thick cloud of dust. At seven the party arrived at what was to have been their overnight stop. The next day's program was to begin in one hour.

This was now Jawaharlal's life. Other men would have crumbled under the killing pace he set for himself. There was unbounded energy and resilience in the slight body. He ate sparingly and often skipped meals completely. But mainly it was the old love affair between him and the Indian masses that refreshed and rejuvenated him.

Election Day came, and Congress basked in the glory of victory. Yet Nehru's double nature remained troubled and restless. Jawaharlal the idol of the masses could never completely vanquish Jawaharlal the lonely aristocratic thinker. Even when he was surrounded by the people, he was not one of them.

"Am I on the way to becoming a selfish demagogue," he pondered in his self-torment, "another one of those unprincipled politicians who use the masses as tools, as stepping-stones to power? Is this how dictators are made?"

In a Calcutta magazine appeared an anonymous article clearly pointing at this danger. After a cruelly sharp analysis of Nehru's personality it concluded:

> . . . He has all the makings of a dictator in him—vast popularity, a strong will, energy, pride—and with all his love of the crowd, an intolerance of others and a certain contempt for the weak and inefficient. His flashes of temper are well known. His overwhelming desire to get things done, to sweep away what he dislikes and build anew, will hardly brook for long the slow process of democracy. . . . His conceit is already formidable. It must be checked. We want no Caesars.

India's intelligentsia buzzed with astonishment. The author seemed to have epitomized him well. Who was the writer anyhow? The most fantastic guesses were advanced, but the publisher remained silent, true to his promise. Years later the author himself revealed his identity to a foreign interviewer. It was Jawaharlal Nehru.

He had been nominated for an unprecedented third term as president of the Indian National Congress. Feeling uneasy about the danger of a one-man rule, he was campaigning against himself, but without success. All rival candidates withdrew, and the vote was unanimous.

The article revealed again Nehru's persistent desire for self-criticism and painful self-analysis. While there is no doubt that he actually possesses many of those dangerous qualities mentioned, he has since proven that he had no intention of becoming an Indian Caesar. "Few men with these talents," concludes one of his biographers, "could have resisted the inducements to exercise dictatorial powers."

The summer of 1938 found him back in Europe. Ostensibly he had gone to visit Indira, who was attending the University of Oxford, but it was also a fact-finding and a propaganda tour. The world saw in him more and more the articulate spokesman of the Indian people.

From the Asian subcontinent he flew straight into Barcelona, Spain, an unhappy city prostrate under the blows of civil war. There he once more met Krishna Menon, who had come from London to report and to receive instructions. Night after night their hotel rocked with the impact of exploding bombs. From the balcony the two friends observed spectacular fires as the armies of the republican government were slowly being crushed and bled dry by the forces of General Franco with the generous support of Hitler and Mussolini.

Deeply disturbed, Jawaharlal moved on to England. From Adolf Hitler came a siren call, an invitation to be the honored guest of the Third Reich. Nehru refused. Instead he went to troubled Czechoslovakia. Hitler had just swallowed the Sudetenland, rich in industry and natural resources, the most valuable section of this democratic country. Now he was getting ready to devour the rest.

The dictators, the saber-rattling militarists, were on the march.

And what were the enlightened Western powers doing, England, France, the United States? They were doing exactly nothing. In fact, they were encouraging the dictators by remaining silent in the face of the rape and destruction of millions of innocent people.

As a son of Asia, Nehru could have felt some satisfaction in seeing the colonial masters, with all their airs of superiority, unable to cope with their own problems. But this was small comfort. It was his world too, the world of Western civilization. His heart bled as he watched darkness settle upon it.

He returned to India, just in time to face more personal tragedy. His mother, already crippled from her long ailment, suffered a paralytic stroke. Through the long night Jawaharlal and his sister Krishna sat by her bedside. Swarup, who was now a provincial minister, came rushing from her post. At five o'clock in the morning life slipped peacefully from the wasted body.

Still restless and dissatisfied with himself and the world, Jawaharlal took off again, this time to China, which was engaged in a fight to death against the Japanese invaders. It was a gesture of sympathy for a nation defending its liberty against heavy odds.

The Japanese war machine had overrun most of China's seacoast where all the important cities were located. The government was operating from a makeshift capital, Chungking, deep in the mountainous interior. Generalissimo and Madame Chiang Kai-shek warmly welcomed the emissary from the other Asian giant. Together they ducked into air-raid shelters in the evening, and next morning viewed the smoking ruins left by Japanese bombers. Jawaharlal took a great liking to the generalissimo, then still widely admired as a leader of gallant resistance against brutal aggression.

Nehru asked himself, "Why is it that the Chinese I see on the debris-littered streets are so exuberant, even cheerful, while Indians often are timid and subdued?"

He thought long. At last he had the answer: "The difference is that Indians are a captive people while the Chinese are free."

After twelve days in China, Nehru was urgently called

home. Hitler's hordes had invaded Poland. The Second World War was on.

What was India to do about the new war in Europe?

Jawaharlal loathed Hitler and all he stood for. Nothing would have pleased him more than to join in the fight. But Gandhi still stood uncompromisingly for nonviolent means. He would not agree with his disciple that passive resistance was of little avail against Nazi dive bombers. On the whole, Nehru's friends failed to understand why he became so excited about events that happened far away and were none of their business.

On the first day of the war the viceroy, Lord Linlithgow, declared, as a matter of course, that India too was now at war. Indian troops were immediately dispatched to Egypt, to Aden, to Singapore.

Nehru would have been in favor of these measures, but he rebelled against the way they were taken. It was for India, not for a heartily disliked stranger, to decide if her sons should fight on distant battlefields. The white sahib in his gilded palace had learned no lesson. All he had to offer was the lame old dictate that in wartime nobody must interfere with the war effort.

With biting irony Nehru pointed out the inconsistency: against Hitler's tyranny Britons expressed revulsion, but they did not see anything wrong in employing much the same methods toward their colonial subjects.

"England is fighting for democracy and freedom," declared the viceroy.

"Whose freedom?" asked Nehru.

Outcries of protest answered the viceroy's declaration. In the provinces, Congress ministers resigned their posts, a step that proved, in the long run, to have been a bad mistake. Both sides were nervous and blundered badly.

In an angry statement, largely from the pen of Nehru, Congress declared:

If Great Britain fights for democracy, then she must necessarily end imperialism in her own possessions and establish full democracy in India. A free and democratic India will gladly associate herself with other free nations for mutual defense against aggression. The true measure of democracy is the ending of imperialism and fascism alike.

Closer and closer to the Indian subcontinent moved the noise of battle. Hitler had overrun a major part of Europe. Then Japan cut loose with her sneak attack on Pearl Harbor. Soon the banner of the Rising Sun fluttered victoriously over all southeast Asia. India herself lay now in the path of the attackers.

Winston Churchill led England in her darkest hour. Every lover of freedom—and that included Jawaharlal Nehru—felt admiration for the old warrior who would fight the Nazis, if need be, "on the beaches, on the landing grounds, in the fields and in the streets," and who pledged, "We shall never surrender."

But the same Churchill also said, "I have not become the King's First Minister in order to preside over the liquidation of the British Empire," and, "We have no intention of casting away that most truly bright and precious jewel in the crown of the King, which more than all our Dominions and Dependencies, constitutes the glory and strength of the British Empire."

Gloom settled over that "bright and precious jewel." As long as Churchill was at the Empire's helm, there was no hope for a change of heart. India was rent by bitter dissension, but on Gandhi's firm insistence, it was decided to carry on the struggle for independence, war or no war, and to launch a new civil disobedience campaign.

Never had Nehru come closer to breaking with the Mahatma, never had the turmoil in his soul raged more intensely. In his anguish he sought temporary escape in the mountains which he loved so much. For two weeks he hiked along the slopes of the beautiful Kulu Valley. His body felt rejuvenated and his nerves calmed, but no real peace came to his groping mind.

By the time he returned, the invasion road to India lay open. Burma had been lost to the Japanese.

Even in defeat, the color line was maintained by the "master race." For generations many hundreds of thousands of Indians had lived inside Burma. Now they fled toward their ancestral land before the Japanese steamroller, through jungles and across mountains, constantly beset by the enemy, by disease and starvation. Stories of flagrant discrimination filtered back to India. Transportation and other assistance were always found for British refugees, but not for Indians. "From one place in Burma," Nehru was told, "where vast numbers of refugees were gathering there were two roads leading to India. The better one was reserved for Britishers or Europeans; it became known as the White Road."

Still he hoped that, in the hour of greatest need, cooperation under honorable conditions could be achieved. He proposed that, in exchange for independence, India would raise an army of five million guerrillas to defend her soil. His offer was turned down.

In the meantime, Gandhi had coined a new slogan, short and commanding, "Quit India." Soon it was shouted in the city bazaars and by the village wells. It was scrawled on walls and scratched in the sand. It screamed from banner headlines in hundreds of newspapers, "Quit India."

Hardly anybody believed that this not too friendly invitation would be heeded. The "Quit India" propaganda was to be the starting signal for a final massive civil disobedience effort. But before it could get under way, the mighty arm of the Empire reached out for the leaders. This was war, a deadly serious war, and the government meant business. On a steamy August morning many thousand Congress volunteers were caught in a country-wide dragnet of police raids. For the ninth time Nehru went to prison. His next three birthdays he was to celebrate during this, his longest term of "rigorous confinement."

The mass arrests brought in their wake mass demonstrations of protest. Harassed by reverses on the battlefield, the authorities struck back brutally. Tight censorship prevented accurate accounts, but it was common knowledge that several thousand Indians had been felled by police bullets and more than one hundred thousand herded into jail.

After this, deadly silence, the silence of the police state, descended upon the land.

In prison Nehru again diverted his frustrated mental energy into literary activity. The result was the book *Discovery of India*, dedicated "To my colleagues and co-prisoners in the Ahmadnagar Fort prison camp from August 9, 1942 to March 28, 1945."

At Ahmadnagar Fort he found himself in the company of men, all high-ranking Congress leaders, who, with their diverse talents and backgrounds, could have staffed the faculty of any first-rate college. Among them were Sanskrit scholars, modern linguists, historians and philosophers. In long conversations with those eleven men, Nehru amassed a huge treasure of knowledge which he skillfully compiled in this account of India's historical fate and culture from dim antiquity to the present.

But all the learned discussion and all the literary work were a poor substitute for freedom of movement. The imprisoned leaders suffered not so much from the petty chicaneries of their jailers, as from the lack of accurate news. There they were, shut away, just when the world was shaken by the most momentous crises. Only through the prison grapevine, after interminable delays, did they learn what course the war was taking:

The Axis onslaught finally brought to a halt—The Allies taking the offensive—Africa cleared of Nazi armies—France reconquered—The Japanese forced into retreat and pushed back to their own islands—The United Nations founded—Germany beaten and broken up—

The earth shook in its foundations. This was the time to shape the new Europe, the new Asia. But Nehru and his friends could only tend the flowers in the tiny prison garden and talk and wait. They were middle-aged men now. Time was running out on them.

Then the war was over, and the prison doors opened.

Out of touch for so long, they haltingly took stock of the situation: the enemy lay smashed. The first atomic bombs had raised their deadly mushroom clouds. A period in the history of war had come to an end.

In the camp of the victors there was no cockiness. The British Empire found itself on the winning side, but it had received such a bloodletting that it was reeling on the brink of ruin. The time had come to retrench. Possession of a vast string of colonies, dispersed all over the globe, had become a luxury England could ill afford.

Churchill was no longer prime minister. The Labor party was in power, eager to shed the costly burden of responsibility for India, the sooner the better.

Day by day, Britain's grasp on the subcontinent was slipping. Indian soldiers and sailors mutinied. Jubilantly they marched through the streets carrying huge "Quit India" banners, while British officials, once so quick with the master's whip, looked on. They marked time, since they knew that their days were numbered.

During the spring of 1946, when Congress met in the city of Karachi, the scent of freedom was in the air. The long, long struggle was drawing to a close.

But among the men in white homespun, the pallor of recent confinement still on their faces, there was little rejoicing. Their shoulders seemed to sag under the prospect of staggering responsibilities about to be thrust upon them. For decades they had been rebels; now they were to rule a vast country rent by inner turmoil, faced with growing Hindu-Moslem antagonism and upset by a ruinous war.

Gravely the chairman gaveled the meeting to order and called for nominations to the office of Congress president. It was an annual routine affair, but now it had taken on special significance. Whoever received the honor this time, would, in all probability, be the first prime minister of a free India. They could ill afford to make a mistake.

Several names were placed in nomination, but only two serious contenders emerged. They were Sardar Patel and Jawaharlal Nehru.

The atmosphere in the halls and cloakrooms was tense. Small groups huddled and argued here and there.

"Patel is in line for the post," contended a number of influential men. "Jawaharlal has been in the chair already three times."

"Patel is the older man," said others. "He deserves the honor. This is in keeping with Indian tradition."

"The leading members in my province have instructed me to vote for Patel." Such statements came from many corners.

Sardar Patel, fifteen years Nehru's senior, was a superb organizer with a genius for getting things done. Of the two he was by far the more skilled practical politician. Theories and philosophical speculations held no attraction for him, but once a line of policy was determined, he was the man to ram it through against all obstacles. On his stocky body sat a formidable bald skull. He was a stubborn, single-minded nationalist, rigidly conservative when it came to social problems. Often he had clashed in heated debate with his liberal-minded younger colleague.

Now Patel faced Nehru in the most critical contest of their careers, and Patel seemed to have the edge.

Then the Mahatma stepped in. Bent and gnarled with age, his body weakened by the many fasts, he was still the conscience of the movement.

Gandhi declared himself for Nehru. With a valiant display of discipline, Patel bowed to his wish and withdrew his candidacy. Seventy-one years old, he knew he would not have another chance. Dutifully he resigned himself to second place, but he never quite forgave Nehru. Their relationship remained strained and wrought with tension till Patel's death in 1950.

Why had Gandhi thrown his weight toward the election of Nehru? He said, "Jawaharlal cannot be replaced today, whilst the charge is being taken from Englishmen. He, a Harrow boy, a Cambridge graduate and a barrister, is wanted to carry on the negotiations with Englishmen."

It was true, Jawaharlal was well versed in the ways of the British, but this could not have been the only reason. Gandhi's keen mind sensed that Nehru was also, next to himself, the Indian best-known around the world. The fledgling government would need his international prestige. Then there was his immense popularity with the masses. Congress needed him to establish rapport with the average Indian. And his progressive philosophy had rallied around him the young intellectuals on whom a self-governing India would have to depend heavily.

Once more Jawaharlal Nehru was acclaimed as president of the Indian National Congress. One month later, the viceroy invited him to form an interim government which was to engineer the complete transfer of power from the British crown to the Indian people.

In fact, though not yet in name, Nehru was now the chief executive of over four hundred million Indians.

At that very moment, the moment of triumph and fulfillment, the new country went insane and began to spill its own blood with the cold fury that only religious fanaticism can generate.

12.

BROTHER AGAINST BROTHER

JAWAHARLAL NEHRU SPENT LONG, hard days negotiating the details of independent India's governmental structure. Seated with him around the conference table were the members of the Cabinet Mission, a delegation of British ministers led by the world-renowned statesman, Sir Stafford Cripps.

On the whole, Jawaharlal found merit in the plan the ministers had brought with them from England: the federal government of India was to have charge of foreign affairs, defense and communications, whereas all other matters would be dealt with by provincial governments. Some provinces would have strong Hindu majorities, others predominantly Moslem populations, but everywhere the rights of the minorities would be guaranteed.

Nehru was still arguing with the British politicians about the composition of an interim cabinet which was to put the whole plan into effect when an urgent message from Calcutta was handed him. He paled and rushed out of the room. The roof was falling in, threatening to pull down the whole structure on which he had been laboring for decades.

He had just learned of the Great Calcutta Killing, as the newspapers were soon to label the dreadful sequence of events.

The air of Calcutta was clammy in the aftermath of heavy monsoon showers. From dirty puddles by the curbstones rose

125

sticky vapors. It was the time of the year when people were most irritable and tempers flared easily.

The high command of the Moslem League had called for mass meetings on August 16, 1946. Obligingly the Moslem-dominated provincial government of Bengal had declared a legal holiday and closed all its operations in Calcutta, the capital of the province and India's largest city.

The Moslems were on the march. They marched eight and ten abreast, their brown faces framed by turbans or topped by brimless fur caps. In enervating monotony rose the rhythmic shout, "Pakistan—Pakistan—Pakistan." From open windows Moslem women, shrouded in veils, screamed encouragement to the marching columns that were to converge on giant Maidan Park in the heart of the city.

In one street the marching ranks suddenly halted. Bodies stiffened, arms flailed the air. Jagged pieces of brick were hurled against a Hindu temple. They were followed by stones wrapped in oil-soaked burning rags. Black smoke billowed into the street.

The mob fanned out, wielding knives and swinging eight-foot clubs. Soon blood trickled from the sidewalks and mingled with the stagnant water in the puddles.

All human restraint had disappeared. From column to column, from street to street spread the madness. A few hours later, the smoke of burning houses and shops hung heavily over the city. Down to the river front stormed the rioters seeking out the clumsy craft on which Hindu families lived and carried cargo. The fire jumped from boat to boat till the debris disappeared hissing in the brackish water.

Buses and streetcars ground to a halt. Two-wheeled rickshas lay overturned in the streets, resting on their drivers whose throats had been cut.

The unprecedented looting, killing and arson went on all day and all night. It continued into the next day and into the one thereafter, as Hindus awoke from their daze and banded together for reprisals. Now mosques and residences in Moslem districts went up in flames. Ugly packs of white-necked vultures picked on bloated bodies that were rapidly decaying in the heat.

Over four thousand people died in the Great Calcutta Killing, and this was only the beginning.

From Calcutta, religious fanaticism carried the flame of violence to city after city, to villages and country cross-roads. Indian turned mercilessly against Indian. Before sanity finally returned to the newly independent country, at least two hundred thousand persons had lost their lives and ten million had barely saved theirs by taking to the highways as refugees.

For Nehru not only did this holocaust spell political defeat, since it buried forever the so carefully worked-out Cabinet Mission Plan; it was also a personal tragedy, worse perhaps—the collapse of a long-cherished philosophy.

He had been reared in an environment of tolerance and broad-mindedness. Moslem friends had always been wel-come in his home; Moslem culture was an important in-gredient of his intellectual background. He had planned, for so many years, to lead an India which would give the world an object lesson in brotherhood, where men of many reli-gions and races and castes would work together in harmony.

And now this. Fury and shame raged inside him. A quarter-century of Gandhi's teachings seemed to be forgotten. Gripped by a feeling of utter futility, he was, for a moment, ready to give up.

Actually, it was one of the major mistakes in Nehru's public career not to have foreseen this nightmare. His deep-seated humanism had blinded him to the cruel realities. He just had not reckoned with the existence of a vast reservoir of primeval hate and destructive force. Composing an ideal future in his active mind, he had forgotten the dismal present.

How could it have happened?

For ages Hindus and Moslems had lived side by side in India. The Mogul rulers whom Jawaharlal's ancestors had served professed Islam. Hindus and Moslems spoke the same language and bargained in the same bazaars. "The Moslem peasantry and industrial workers are hardly distinguishable from the Hindu," wrote Nehru in one of his books. According to him, religious separatism was preached only by the most backward-looking elements in both groups.

Isolated incidents occurred, however. During festivals Hindus liked to parade through the streets with music and lots of noise. Wedding parties resounded with bells and cymbals. Moslems became infuriated when such merry-making occurred in front of their mosques at prayer time. On the other hand, Hindu tempers flared when Moslems were seen butchering cows which are sacred according to the Brahman religion. But such quarrels were of short duration and soon forgotten.

Moslems joined the Congress movement in significant numbers. Quite a few rose to high offices. Several served as presidents. One prominent Congress Moslem was Mohammed Ali Jinnah who, almost singlehandedly, was to break India into two and create Pakistan.

Thirteen years older than Nehru, Jinnah also was an English-trained lawyer from a wealthy family. He was always immaculately dressed, after the latest European fashion, and he sported a monocle, the symbol of European upper-crust haughtiness. His unbelievably thin, almost fleshless frame, topped by a head with leathery sunken cheeks and bright, burning eyes, was a sight few people could ever forget.

In the early years of the movement, when Nehru was still a shy, pretty unknown backbencher, Jinnah, ironically, was an ardent spokesman of Hindu-Moslem unity. He was filled with limitless ambition, and his career as a Congress politician seemed assured. But when Gandhi appeared on the scene, he raised his aristocratic nose in disdain. This new catering to the common man was not for him. While Nehru drew new strength and inspiration from his contacts with the peasant, Jinnah shuddered at the sight of the ill-groomed plain people who now began to crowd into Congress meetings. He could hardly understand their talk.

Everything in him rebelled against Gandhi's tactics. No, police batons and filthy prisons were not for him. "The enthusiasm of the people struck him as mob hysteria," remarked Nehru who, with his keen talent of observation, was following the course of the older colleague's career with great interest.

Gradually Jinnah drifted away from the independence movement, realizing that now his type of personality had little chance of being properly appreciated. He returned to England. There he was approached by an emissary from the Moslem League asking him to take over its leadership. As Congress had been before Gandhi, the Moslem League was then a lusterless, rather aimless and definitely leaderless group of wealthy conservatives. Founded in 1906, it was hardly known among the Islamic rank and file.

Jinnah saw his opportunity. He rushed back to India. In an amazingly short time he had become the undisputed dictator of the Moslem League. In his unbearably domineering way, loved by nobody, but feared by many, he welded it into a disciplined instrument of his boundless ambition.

Nehru who had, in the meantime, moved into the front ranks of Congress leadership listened with growing amazement as Jinnah now raised his voice louder and louder to demand special privileges for the Moslems in a liberated India. Trying to preserve the unity of the independence movement, Nehru approached the Moslem leader many times, pleading with him not to obstruct the common cause. But Jinnah kept raising the price for cooperation till further negotiations had become pointless.

Nehru should have been forewarned, yet he was dumfounded, as were most of his friends, when Jinnah, in 1940, proclaimed the "Two Nation Theory." "India," he thundered, "is not a nation at all, just a geographic term. Hindus and Moslems represent two distinct nations. They must have two separate countries." A united independent India, he reasoned, would actually be a Hindu country. The Moslems would remain an oppressed minority. Their new masters might even turn out to be more brutal than the old ones.

"We must have our own government," he cried. "We must have Pakistan."

Mohammed Ali Jinnah went about his task with deadly efficiency. The icy, humorless squire became a skilled agitator, playing on the fanaticism of the easily aroused Moslem masses. Soon he was hailed by his followers as the *Quaid-i-Azam* (Savior of the People).

Almost to the end Nehru made the fatal mistake of underestimating Jinnah. His intense dislike for any division along religious lines clouded his judgment. Wishfully he believed that the Moslem League furor would soon subside and that Jinnah would, in the end, be open to friendly reasoning as one could expect from an intelligent gentleman with a Western education. Nehru failed to fully measure the burning drive in his power-hungry former colleague who now saw himself in possession of a most formidable tool: the blind allegiance of millions bound together by violent emotion.

The final deliberations for the British withdrawal began. But there stood the seventy-year-old Moslem leader, obstructing, threatening, barring the way to a peaceful take-over. It was chiefly his doing that the Cabinet Mission Plan failed.

The interim government headed by Nehru was boycotted by the League at every turn. One of its resolutions read, "Moslems will resist such a government with their blood." Five ministerial posts had been reserved for Jinnah's men, but they refused to attend cabinet meetings. League representatives also failed to take their seats in the Constituent Assembly of India.

Disturbed, but determined, Nehru went ahead with final plans for independence. It was then that Jinnah proclaimed Direct Action Day. "Today," he declared, "we bid good-by to constitutional methods." Officially it was a call for public demonstrations, but to the aroused Moslem masses it sounded very much like a call to arms.

Finally shocked out of his misplaced optimism when the first reports of atrocities began pouring in, Nehru tried a final approach. He rushed to Bombay where Jinnah had his home. For hours he pleaded with his adversary to use restraint in his proclamations, to curb the fanaticism of his followers rather than inflame it further. Jinnah listened politely. His short answers were correct and clipped, but Nehru's appeal made no impact. The *Quaid-i-Azam* did nothing to stem the flood after he had opened the floodgates.

The outburst of unrestrained violence, whether deliberately brought about or not, had the desired effect. The British had long harbored tender feelings toward the Moslem League because it opposed Congress. Now they declared themselves in favor of partition as a way to prevent complete chaos. Even some Congress leaders began to wonder whether large-scale civil disorder was not too high a price to pay for political unity.

A new viceroy was sent from London, the last in the long line of men representing the British crown. Lord Mountbatten's mission was to engineer Britain's withdrawal and to terminate his own job. A cool, seasoned tactician and realist, he wanted to accomplish this in the shortest possible time and with the least outlay of human lives.

Watching the holocaust of riot and counterriot around him, he soon embraced the idea of Pakistan as the only practical solution. Shrewdly he set out to sell this point of view to the Congress high command and especially to its president.

Nehru switched positions only after another of his many inner struggles. "By cutting off the head," he finally comforted himself, "we shall get rid of the headache."

His acceptance of the Pakistan solution was in no small way a result of his friendship with Lord and Lady Mountbatten. Both the last British viceroy and the first Indian prime minister were at heart refined English gentlemen, and they were also progressive thinkers with great sympathies for the underdog. They thought similar thoughts and expressed them in the same impeccable language. Lady Mountbatten added her considerable charm to this warm personal relationship. The lonely widower, tormented by his doubts and weary of all the political intriguing, liked to relax in the friendly atmosphere of the viceregal residence, where he was a frequent visitor.

Gandhi refused to the bitter end to accept the idea of partition, but nobody else wanted to wait. Congress leadership, so long excluded from the inner chambers of government, was anxious to taste the sweet fruits of power. In this one instance they ignored the Mahatma's counsel.

The night came when the conch shell was blown and the fireworks crackled over the streets of New Delhi. Jawaharlal Nehru stood before the Constituent Assembly and proclaimed the birth of the Indian nation. But it was now a diminished, a truncated nation, for Pakistan had declared its independence only a few hours earlier.

For Nehru his new country was still India, not a Hindu nation, but the home of many nationalities and religions from which, unfortunately, a sizable minority had decided to secede.

Partition, however, did not bring an end to the eternal slaughter. As so often before, the Mahatma's counsel proved, in the end, to have been right. In 1948, looking back on the tragic months that followed partition, Nehru himself was to write, "We consented because we thought we were purchasing peace and good will, though at a high price. . . . I do not know, if I had the same choice, how I would decide."

It was one thing to agree on a separate state for Moslems and quite another to draw up exact boundary lines. In fact, it proved impossible. To this day about ten million Hindus

live in Pakistan and over forty million Moslems in India.
Besides, a large number of Sikhs, a colorful offshoot of Hinduism with a long history of violent quarrels with Islam, found
themselves suddenly within Pakistan.

Then the carnage erupted on an unprecedented scale. The
Calcutta Killing had only been a warm-up. In Pakistan irate
Moslems turned on their Hindu and Sikh neighbors in an
orgy of murder, rape and arson. On the other side of the
artificial dividing line, Hindus and Sikhs retaliated with
equal ferocity. Caravans of refugees, at times fifty miles long,
wound across the bleeding country. They walked barefoot
or rode on bullock carts, dragging along their old, their
children and a few miserable belongings. Others crowded
into trains, perched on the roofs of the coaches and hung
from running boards and couplings. Armed gangs attacked
the caravans, littering the highways with corpses. Trains
arrived at stations with blood running from doors and
windows.

Those who survived brought with them the bitter seed
of hatred.

Hardly formed, the new government of India faced the
task of caring for countless refugees cramped into tent cities
in public parks and empty lots or just bedding down for
the night on the sidewalks. Still groping for a firm footing,
the national leadership braced itself for the fight against
starvation and epidemics, for the control of fanaticism and
revenge.

In those days the stature of Jawaharlal Nehru grew until
it assumed the proportions of greatness. "It was he alone,"
admitted one of his bitterest critics, "who held the nation
together in the tragic aftermath of partition."

With the jubilant shouts of his admirers still ringing in
his ears, he hurried away from the independence celebrations. Closeted with his aides, he spent day and night fighting
against civil war. Like a general in the field, he kept a huge

war map in his office with pins being moved around on it to show the shifting centers of gravest disturbance. What meager and overworked police forces he had available he rushed to those spots.

From his residence issued a continuous stream of orders opening up stores of food, commandeering shelters and medical service for the refugees. His voice became familiar to radio listeners as he admonished them in endless repetition, "Our first and immediate objective must be to put an end to all the eternal strife and violence which disfigure and degrade us and injure the cause of freedom."

His friends worried because he looked weary and haggard, but he shook off the benumbing fog of exhaustion and took again to the road. He traveled through the worst riot-ridden areas in the Punjab, completely disregarding any caution. In a makeshift hospital he bent over a child whose hands had been chopped off. In a crib a baby cried, the sole survivor of a large family that had been wiped out on its flight across the border.

He visited a camp of Moslems who had fled from their isolated homes and huddled together to seek safety in each other's company. "Forget the past," he pleaded with them. "Extend the hand of brotherhood to your neighbors. The new India needs all of you."

From there he rushed to a makeshift camp of Hindu refugees recently arrived from Pakistan. They had seen him come from the Moslem encampment. Eyes filled with hate greeted him. Fists were raised. "Traitor," he heard them cry. "Betrayer of Hindus. Go to your Moslem friends."

His companions feared a shower of stones or the thrust of a sharp knife, but Nehru marched on unmoved. At the central gathering place he turned and faced the crowd. They fell silent. Those closest to him fell back a few steps. The words came from his dry mouth rasping and hoarse:

"You have shouted, '*Mahatma Gandhi ki jai*,' haven't you? And now what are you doing? You have dishonored the

Mahatma. Is this how responsible citizens of a free country behave? You are not worthy of *swaraj*—"

They hung their heads like naughty children caught in the midst of their mischief.

From the country he rushed back to Delhi, where Moslem-hunting had become a cruel sport, just in sight of the government buildings. In the old section of the capital city, he led the police personally, like a supercharged bulldozer, into the midst of the rioting. "Confiscate all weapons," he screamed at the policemen who stood around hesitant to manhandle their countrymen and coreligionists. "Take everything: clubs, knives, daggers."

He moved deeper into the bedlam, pushing aside the looters as he went. They looked at him, grinned and went on with their job. He threatened, but they mockingly shoved him out of the way.

"Out with your pistols," he bellowed at the outnumbered policemen. "Don't you see? Crimes are being committed. What are you here for?" Still they demurred.

"You heard me." shouted the prime minister at the top of his voice. "You know your duty. Now fulfill it or quit the service."

The weapons came out of the holsters. Shots rang out, and bullets whistled above the heads of the looters. The mob fell back.

Nehru moved on. A howling mass had surrounded a house. Knives flashed in bloodstained hands. Eyes full of murder were focused on the roof where some movement could be seen. The prime minister rushed up a rickety flight of stairs and found at the top two Moslem children, paralyzed with fear. Carrying the smaller one in his arm and holding the other by the hand, Nehru led them down the stairs and out of the house. A lane opened reluctantly, and he took the children past a wall of clenched teeth and smoldering eyes to a waiting police van.

Almost the whole first year of independence went by before the fire of madness and wanton destruction slowly burned itself out. Only then could the prime minister and his government turn from fire-fighting to the task of building India's future.

13.

THE LIGHT GOES OUT

AT ONE TIME ANCIENT ROME was jointly ruled by three men. This was called the "triumvirate." During the first year of India's independence, many observers also spoke of a triumvirate, though it was of a quite different nature. The three men who then kept the heavily rolling ship afloat were: Prime Minister Jawaharlal Nehru, the voice of India, the mastermind and planner; Deputy Prime Minister Sardar Patel, the wily boss of Congress, who kept the machinery of government oiled and running; Mohandas K. Gandhi, seventy-eight years old, the spiritual father of the new nation, a private citizen without any official government position.

The team faced tremendously difficult tasks for which there was no precedent, no manual of instructions.

The intricate web of the old colonial government had to be disentangled and the strands carefully divided between the new India and the new Pakistan. The old British officers' corps was split down the middle and partially moved to Karachi, the Pakistani capital; and all the contents of the former colonial offices, down to typewriters, desks, chairs and even pencils, were meticulously separated. Pakistan even received its share of inmates from the colonial penitentiaries and insane asylums.

Nehru's India came out by far the better of the two countries. New Delhi, capital of the former crown colony and now the capital of the new nation, was already a going concern. A cluster of government buildings was ready for the new occupants, many of whom possessed long experience as civil servants. The core of police and army, of judges and provincial administrators, also continued on from the former regime.

A matter of the utmost urgency was the liquidation of the six hundred princely states that dotted the map of India like flyspecks. Their rulers, the maharajas, were rich in palaces, diamonds and caparisoned elephants, but the states in which lived almost one-fourth of India's population were among the most backward and mismanaged areas.

Nehru had often hurled accusing words at the princes and at the British government that coddled them and turned deaf ears to the criticism of progressive voices everywhere. The maharajas were puppets who did not mind the strings pulled by the puppeteers in London, since they were granted an almost completely free hand in the internal affairs of their states, which they ruled as typical oriental despots. Of course, they were hostile to the independence movement that was bound to upset their cozy establishments.

The maharajas varied greatly in importance and character. One state was the size of France while others were not bigger than an average farm. The largest had over sixteen million inhabitants, the smallest less than one thousand. Some rulers were enlightened and dedicated statesmen while the majority, though immensely rich, left their subjects to vegetate in hopeless filth and misery.

Now the maharajas were given the choice of turning their lands over to either India or Pakistan.

It was in those delicate political maneuvers that Patel showed his unmatched skill as a negotiator. In an unbelievably short time most princely states were incorporated into India. The princes were naturally reluctant to give up their parasitic existence, but they saw the handwriting on the wall. The British bayonets had kept them on their gilded thrones. Once those bayonets were gone, their own fate would be sealed.

The government was very generous in settling with the princes. They could keep their considerable private fortunes and were given liberal pensions which, in some cases, amounted to two million dollars annually.

Only one maharaja delayed his exit long enough to provoke a dangerous crisis. That was the ruler of Kashmir. He was a Hindu, but the majority of his subjects were Moslems. While he was ineptly playing for time, tough Pathan tribesmen from the wild western mountains invaded Kashmir in force. It is now pretty well established that those raids were encouraged by the Pakistani government. The Moslem Pathans advanced on Srinagar, the capital of Kashmir, but they stopped along the way to loot and rape and, more often than not, to kill. Whether the victims were Hindus, Sikhs or Moslems made little difference to them.

It was only then that the maharaja decided to turn his tortured country over to India and, at the same time, to ask Nehru urgently for military help.

From the mountain world of Kashmir, Nehru's ancestors once descended into the Indian plains. To its valleys and ridges he returned as often as he could for precious holidays of hiking and climbing. Deep emotional attachment tied him to this far corner of the peninsula.

Again conflicting sentiments raged in his mind. India needed peace and friendship more than she needed additional territory. But Kashmir is a strategic gateway to three foreign countries, the Soviet Union, China and Afghanistan, and leaving it in Moslem hands might have brought on another bloody wave of religious rioting at home.

In the end the prime minister accepted Kashmir into the Indian nation and declared it to be under the protection of his government. In a matter of hours, Indian troops were on their way to the trouble spots in a daring airlift over foggy mountains with visibility almost zero. In short order the troops cleared the greater part of Kashmir. In their first test under fire, India's soldiers acquitted themselves nobly.

Since then Kashmir has remained a point of bitter contention between Pakistan and India, a constant source of irritation that has, at times, led to the brink of open warfare. An uneasy truce prevails whereby India controls about two-thirds and Pakistan the remainder of the former princely state.

During those critical months, the "triumvirate" appeared to the outside world as a harmonious group. But though all three men knew the absolute necessity of unity, tension developed. Occasional rumors of an imminent break between Nehru and Patel swirled around the capital.

When the colonial treasure was to be divided between the two successor governments, Patel wanted to keep all the funds in New Delhi; otherwise Pakistan's share might be used to fight India. Nehru and Gandhi, however, insisted that Pakistan receive its full share despite the bad blood over Kashmir. Practical politics clashed head-on with broader legal and moral principles.

Gandhi had moved to the capital where G. D. Birla, a wealthy industrialist, offered him the hospitality of his palatial residence. There the Mahatma spent his days meditating in a simple room or walking in the lush gardens. The prime minister paid almost daily calls. No important matter was decided upon without consultation with *Bapu* (father). To him Nehru confided his innermost thoughts, his doubts, his uncertainties, and he always left Birla House comforted and strengthened. "It was as if going to see *Bapu* were the solution to his dilemma and his weariness," wrote Jawaharlal's niece, "as if the presence of *Bapu* would in itself answer questions and heal wounds."

On January 12, 1948, Gandhi began a fast. "I will not take nourishment till Moslems can walk safely in the streets of Delhi," he declared. "Hindus, Sikhs and Moslems must live as brothers."

Within hours the wires hummed with the news. The national cabinet made it its top agenda. It was discussed in temples and mosques. Many fasted in sympathy, among them a detachment of police on active duty with their British officers. Nehru refused food for one day, then told a mass meeting, "Save the Master's life. The loss of the Mahatma would mean the loss of India's soul."

In the streets Hindus began to talk to Moslems. Responsible citizens of both religions formed joint committees. "What can we do?" they asked each other. "And how can we do it quickly before it is too late?"

Six days after he had last taken nourishment, Gandhi lay on an enclosed porch of Birla House, too weak to talk or move. Relatives and friends squatted in silence around his mat. Outside an endless stream of followers paraded by the windows, trying to detect a sign of life in the emaciated body. Many wept.

There was a stir, and eyes turned toward the porch steps. The prime minister strode up leading several men. The different styles of their clothing and headgear indicated that they were Hindus, Sikhs and Moslems. Nehru bent and spoke into the Mahatma's ear:

"*Bapuji*, they are a delegation of the people of Delhi. The attacks have ceased. Moslems walk freely in the streets. They are pledging themselves to peace and brotherhood."

A white-bearded Sikh held up a sheaf of papers so that the Mahatma's eyes could focus on the many signatures that covered them. "We need you," said a Moslem delegate. "India needs you alive."

The parchment skin tightly drawn over Gandhi's cheekbones creased into a weak smile. A gleam came into his eyes as he signaled one of the women in the room. She brought a cup of diluted fruit juice and held it to his bloodless lips. A deep sigh of relief, almost a groan, rose from the onlookers as the Mahatma broke his fast.

Two days later he resumed his daily prayer meetings in the garden. At the stroke of five, as the gentle rays of the winter sun caressed the treetops for the last time, he was

led from the pavilion by his two granddaughters. Leaning
heavily on the young women, he hobbled to a terrace of
mossy brick that was surrounded by greenery.

Though no announcement had been made, the word had
spread somehow, and the garden was densely filled. Silently
Hindus and Moslems, Brahmins and Untouchables sat side
by side on the lawn. Beyond the low stone wall stood many
more in the streets that surrounded Birla's home.

Soft chanting broke the silence. Somebody recited an old
Sanskrit hymn. Others hummed along. Most remained quiet.
Then Gandhi spoke. It was not a prepared sermon. Rather
he seemed to think out aloud—bursts of thought between
long pauses. His words were of the oneness of God, the like-
ness of all ways to worship Him.

Suddenly an ugly noise rent the serene evening calmness.
It was something terribly out-of-place. Smoke rose from the
edge of the terrace. An acrid smell had extinguished the
scent of flowers. A young man rushed toward the gate, but
a woman barred his way and wrestled with him till others
came running. Severals pairs of arms held him pinned.

A bomb had been thrown intended for the Mahatma. An
angry murmur, like the growl of a wild beast, rose from
the crowd.

Gandhi was unperturbed. "Don't harm him," shrilled his
high-pitched voice. "No violence in this place of peace."

The attacker was led away by a policeman. He was a
Hindu refugee from Pakistan. In his pocket was later found
a hand grenade.

Upon hearing the news the prime minister rushed to Birla
House. *"Bapuji,* you are in danger," he pleaded. "Give up
those prayer meetings for a while."

"No," was the Mahatma's answer. "Many people come.
They need me. I must not disappoint them."

"At least let me arrange for better protection. We'll have
a police cordon around the garden. The visitors will be

searched as they enter. A bodyguard will be stationed on the terrace."

Again the Mahatma shook his head. "Don't fret on my account, Jawaharlal. If I have to die by an assassin's hand, I must do so without anger and fear. I am in God's hand."

Nehru was exasperated. Without Gandhi's knowledge he posted plain-clothes detectives on the scene. But the open garden with its many shrubs, with people everywhere, was a security officer's nightmare.

Tragedy was in the air. The bomb-thrower belonged to a secret organization of Hindu fanatics who wanted a free hand in terrorizing the Moslems in their midst. Gandhi was the strongest obstacle to their goals. Frustrated at every turn, they had sworn, "Gandhi must go."

Informers kept Nehru abreast of the conspiracy. He knew that his name also was on the blacklist. They wanted India to be a Hindu state with the Hindu religion dominant and all others suppressed. This, of course, went against the very grain of Nehru's thinking.

Gandhi continued his prayer meetings.

Ten days after the bomb incident, on the thirtieth of January, the garden was again crowded at sunset. A clock nearby struck five. The Mahatma was always a model of punctuality. To let people wait, he felt, was tactless and overbearing. But on that evening he was nowhere in sight. A surprised murmur floated along the pebble pathways.

Gandhi was still in his room, and with him was Sardar Patel, the deputy prime minister. Again the two leading statesmen had clashed, and sharp words had been exchanged. It all stemmed from a speech Patel had recently made questioning the loyalty of the forty-five million Moslems inside India. "We can't trust any of them," he had shouted, "unless they come forward, one by one, and profess their allegiance to this country."

Nehru had been furious. For him there was only one class

of citizens. No special pledges should be demanded from anybody.

Gandhi was scolding Patel as if he were a naughty school-boy. "You have been with me for thirty years, but you have learned nothing."

The deputy prime minister defended himself: "You know nothing about practical politics, *Bapuji*. This is a time for tough realism, not for lofty dreams."

In the end, as always, Patel submitted to the Mahatma's urging.

The crowd fell silent as the Mahatma finally appeared in the garden. A young man, his features tense, his lips tightly drawn, stepped into his path and offered the traditional *namaste* greeting, folding his hands and bowing slightly. As Gandhi responded with a like gesture, the youth pulled a small revolver from the folds of his loose garment and fired three shots. Two entered the Mahatma's chest, the third his abdomen. He fell with the words, *"Hé Ram"* (O God) on his lips. By the time they had carried him to his room he was dead.

The assassin lifted the pistol to his own head, but he was quickly seized. The bullet only grazed him.

For some time there was stunned silence. Then an outcry rose from hundreds of lips, almost at the same instant. The shrill wailing of female voices spread the word to the on-lookers in the surrounding streets, and on it went through the city, the country, the world, "The Mahatma is dead."

Nehru's face was like a white mask as he arrived from his home. He wept uncontrollably.

Lord Mountbatten, the governor general, rushed to the scene. As he made his way through the vast throng that had gathered, someone asked him, "Who did it, a Hindu or a Moslem?"

He did not know the answer at that time, but without hesitation he said, "A Hindu." The opposite answer might have touched off the most horrible bloodbath in India's history. Fortunately the answer turned out to be correct.

As he entered the chamber, squatting women chanted softly, *"Ram-Ram-Ram,"* Gandhi's last word.

Nehru and Patel were kneeling by the body.

"His last wish was," said the governor general, "that you two should get along and work harmoniously for the welfare of your country."

The two men stood up. A dead silence suddenly hung over the crowded room. They looked at the body at their feet and then at each other. Silently they embraced in a sacred pledge to their dead spiritual master.

During the next three years, till Patel's death, they kept their wordless vow. They had their differences of opinion, but, as Nehru phrased it, "It is odd—the memory of Gandhi keeps us together."

Now the prime minister stepped out into the garden facing the masses that stood in solid ranks as far as the eye could see.

"Mahatmaji is gone." His voice was choked with grief. "The light has gone out of our lives, and there is darkness everywhere. Our beloved leader, *Bapu,* as we called him, the Father of the Nation, is no more—"

Among the many masterful speeches of Nehru's career this was the most moving. It came straight from a bleeding heart.

Later, before the Constituent Assembly, his grief turned to self-accusation:

"I have a sense of utter shame both as an individual and as the head of the government of India that we should have failed to protect the greatest treasure that we possessed."

Then he roused himself from his dejection and continued with a firm voice, "He would chide us if we merely mourn: that is a poor way of doing homage to him. The only way is to express our determination and dedicate ourselves to the great task which he undertook and which he accomplished to such a large extent."

As to the question of a fitting monument, Nehru felt that

it must consist of work and personal sacrifice. He rejected as completely inadequate any memorial "in bronze or marble or pillars."

Next day untold thousands lined the streets, as the funeral procession wound its way over a six-mile route to the river-bank. Many shook their heads in disapproval as they saw the martyred Mahatma's body being borne on a gun carriage. These military trappings seemed strangely out of place at the last rites for the apostle of peace and nonviolence.

Shrouded in the simple homespun that had covered it in life, the body was placed high on the pyre of sandalwood. Nehru stepped up, bowed low and kissed the feet of his departed *guru* in the traditional gesture of farewell. Then, with a flaring torch, Gandhi's son lit the pyre.

Later in the day a boat glided silently into the river. As the ashes were immersed in the sacred waters, many-colored blossoms showered from airplanes circling high above.

A few months before the Mahatma's death, Jawaharlal Nehru, prime minister of India and world-renowned states-man, had written to him, "I know that we must learn to rely upon ourselves and not to run to you for help on every occasion."

Now there would be no more running to *Bapu*. Instead, when faced with important decisions, India's leader could only ask himself, "What would Gandhi have said?"

14.

MR. PRIME MINISTER

GANDHI WAS DEAD, his memory revered in many countries as that of a twentieth-century saint. The thin brown face with the gray mustache and the steel-rimmed glasses had become a lasting world-wide symbol of love and compassion.

But now India needed, more than ever, a living leader who could guide the infant nation in its first uncertain steps and also represent it with effectiveness and dignity to the outside world. Frightening in its complexity and difficulty was the job of Jawaharlal, the Mahatma's disciple and chosen successor.

The prime minister had to tear himself away from the manifold tasks at home to meet his colleagues from other countries on the slippery parqueted floors of international gatherings. The statesmen were curious. How would this man from southern Asia go about his tasks? What figure would he cut in the intricate diplomatic game? How would he address demanding Western audiences? The tests were quick in coming.

In November 1948 Nehru was in Paris addressing the United Nations General Assembly. His strong commitment to the cause of international cooperation made a deep impression on the delegates, who hailed him as the "Voice of the New Asia." Still strikingly handsome, flashing his white teeth frequently in his famous infectious smile, he charmed everybody who came in contact with him.

The whole concept of the United Nations struck a very

147

sympathetic chord in Nehru's heart. Since it fitted so closely into his own ideals and hopes, he saw to it that India had a prominent part in all UN undertakings, from furnishing soldiers for the various police forces to filling the president's chair in the General Assembly (held by Madame Pandit in 1953–54.)

As India's chief delegate to the UN the prime minister chose Krishna Menon, who had returned home from his London outpost after independence was achieved. Soon Nehru's old friend became well-known in the corridors and galleries of the United Nations, but far from well-liked. From 1946 to 1960 he treated this international body to his peculiar brand of irritation. When he limped on his cane into the meeting hall, his dark features crowned by a carefully groomed shock of gray hair, reporters got their pencils ready, for they could always count on some sensational performance. His sarcastic barbs made good copy, and he managed propitious fainting spells, always being sure in advance that photographers were at hand.

But the troublesome Krishna Menon was an ever-faithful mouthpiece of his master's thoughts, often freeing him from the necessity of making some unpopular pronouncement. He also proved to be an extremely skilled negotiator. Many drafts of important resolutions show his skilled hand, such as the compromise that ended the Korean War in 1953 by dividing the country into a northern Communist and a southern non-Communist half. Once he made himself very useful by achieving the release of American airmen held prisoner by the Chinese Reds.

But this service to the United States was overshadowed by his usual obnoxious behavior. His most biting thrusts of sarcasm seemed often aimed at the United States. This reflected, of course, Nehru's own attitude, though the prime minister himself always showed considerably more tact and wisdom in his utterances.

Somehow, Nehru and the United States had, for a number

of years, a hard time understanding each other. A rumor has it that one of his English governesses impressed upon young Jawaharlal the notion that Americans were all ill-bred, uncivilized upstarts. "They have poor table manners," she lectured him, "and their speech is atrocious though they call it English."

The years of study in England fortified this typical prejudice. Even during the Second World War when he met many Americans stationed in India, they seemed to him always "in a hurry and they disregarded old established rules of proper behavior."

Nehru was well read in the history of the American Revolution, which inspired him greatly, but he did not know the Western Hemisphere at first hand. Not before 1949 could he arrange his first visit to the United States. He sought food, for India was then in the throes of famine, but when Congress made the shipment of 2,000,000 tons of wheat dependent on several important concessions, he refused. The wheat came anyhow, eighteen months later, after starvation had taken a heavy toll of human lives. The whole episode left a bitter taste in the prime minister's mouth.

During his visit a group of New York businessmen and corporation presidents gave a dinner in his honor at the Waldorf-Astoria Hotel. Looking around the room, his table neighbor asked him, "Do you realize that you are having dinner with twenty billion dollars?"

At the time, this remark struck the disciple of Gandhi and of the Fabian Socialists as characteristic of gross American materialism.

His view of American ways, based on misunderstanding and lack of contact, did not prevent Nehru from forming many personal friendships with American scholars and statesmen. The United States furnished some of the most prominent experts who helped the Indian government plan its great breakthrough into a better future.

What mainly prevented closer ties between India and

America were the conflicting attitudes toward the realities of the cold war. In 1945, when the Second World War came to an end, militant fascism lay broken on the blood-soaked ground. But into the vacuum sprang totalitarian communism. The United States found itself, almost against its will, responsible for the security of the free world. Some American spokesmen began to press other countries to take a stand in this battle of nerves and propaganda. "Whoever is not for us," they said, "is against us." According to them, nations that refused to join the American defensive alliances, such as the Southeast Asia Treaty Organization, did not deserve their trust and friendship.

This line of thought did not sit well at all with Nehru. Against the pressure to commit his country to either the Western or the Soviet power bloc, he raised the banner of "nonalignment." He began to preach his brand of neutrality with a near-religious fervor. In this world, he felt, there must be room for more than just one point of view, and they should all be able to coexist peacefully. He dramatized his point on a European trip in 1955 when he first paid a friendly visit to Soviet Russia and then flew straight from the Kremlin to Rome, where he called with equal cordiality on the Pope.

There were many reasons for keeping India out of the cold war. All Nehru's plans for economic growth depended on nonalignment. Tied to one of the feuding blocs, the country would have been forced to spend on arms and soldiers what he wanted it to spend on dams, highways and health centers.

By neglecting to build up India's armed forces he wanted to demonstrate the country's complete peacefulness and also his complete trust in her neighbors. Gandhi's great method of moral teaching by example, he felt, could also be applied to foreign relations.

Nehru dreamed of being the mediator between the two

giant antagonists of the cold war, and this role suited him admirably, for he always cherished compromise. "Speak softly," he counseled the statesmen of the world. "Violent gestures and threats of retribution only hinder peaceful solutions." A gentleman himself, he could not see why everybody should not talk and deport himself in a gentlemanly way. "For Nehru," wrote Chester Bowles, American ambassador to India, "the world is not painted in harshly contrasting black and white, but in many subtly interwoven shades of gray."

In the forties and fifties, India's chief executive gained a considerable reputation around the world as a peacemaker and a soother of troubled waters. The biggest names on the international scene were constantly beating a path to his door. But Western statesmen, especially Americans, had much to grumble about, for Nehru's neutrality often showed greater friendliness toward the Communist bloc than toward the free world.

"Why does he find fault only with us?" asked Westerners in their disappointment. "Doesn't he know what goes on behind the Iron Curtain? Or does he not want to know?"

This complaint appeared entirely justified from the Western point of view, yet there was another side to the problem. One must remember that all the former colonial rulers came from the West. Any move in Europe or America that could, even in the remotest way, be interpreted as helpful to colonialism roused Indian tempers to white heat. "I do not know," Nehru pointed out, "if it is adequately realized in many Western countries how strongly we feel on the question of colonialism. It is in our blood—"

American military alliances with weaker Asian and African countries were interpreted by Indian leaders as a new, thinly disguised form of colonial imperialism, especially since several of these alliances included Pakistan. When the United States shipped large quantities of arms to the Pakistanis,

intended for defense against possible Communist attacks,
Nehru became worried lest they be used against India. The
festering hostility of the two neighbors over the Kashmir
issue had frustrated many attempts at better understanding
between India and the West.

Strange as it seems, Nehru's occasional harsh criticism of
America revealed a sense of closeness rather than hostility.
A democratic society, he felt, was accustomed to conflicting
points of view and would not resent a frank exchange of
opinion. On the other hand, totalitarian powers have little
love of those who point at their weaknesses. And there is
always the uncomfortable geographic fact that both the Soviet
Union and Red China hover close to the Indian border like
giant vultures.

While Americans seemed to get under his skin at times,
Nehru had little trouble getting along with the British. With
the struggle for independence out of the way, he saw no
more reason for denying his kind feelings toward the Anglo-
Saxon nation whose writers and thinkers he had learned to
admire so much.

Jawaharlal had once bitterly quarreled with his father,
who wanted to retain some ties with the Empire. But on
Independence Day he enthusiastically proclaimed India's
bonds with the Commonwealth.

Since 1948 Nehru has participated regularly in the deliberations of the Commonwealth prime ministers, and his
voice has commanded increasing respect. He gave the whole
structure a new direction. Most likely, he has kept it from
falling apart.

Upon his suggestion the name of the old British Commonwealth of Nations was changed and the word "British"
dropped to soothe the feelings of radical Indian nationalists.
While other dominions recognize the queen as their nominal
head of state, India, a republic, sees in her only a "symbol"
of Commonwealth unity. The different wording has in no

way harmed the queen's popularity in India. It is probably the only republic in the world that regularly celebrates a royal birthday. The queen's anniversary is an occasion for big parades and much public merrymaking.

When Elizabeth II visited New Delhi in the winter of 1961, over a million cheering Indians lined the streets, and British flags fluttered from buildings and posts and even from donkey and camel carts. "It was the grandest welcome ever extended a visitor," found the prime minister.

The bulk of India's trade is still with the Commonwealth countries. More Britishers do business in Indian cities than ever in the days of the *raj*, and they are well liked. The new country's laws and administration are tailored after the British model.

The coming of India's independence was an inspiration to nationalists all over the old colonial areas, and Nehru became their hero, a spokesman of the hopes and dreams in the hearts of dark-skinned people from the Atlantic to the China Sea. Nehru took to this role of Afro-Asian messiah with great gusto and also with imposing moral strength. From the early days of his regime he sought to rally the awakening colonies around India and help them in their own struggle for independence.

Mainly upon his urging, a unique gathering took place in the Indonesian city of Bandung. There met in 1955 the representatives of twenty-nine nations, all located in Asia or Africa and most of them until recently colonies of Western powers. While the Bandung Conference did not result in any immediate earth-shaking action, it did call world attention to the fact that untold millions who had lived in bondage so long were now free and wanted to be heard and respected. To Nehru, leader of the largest former colony and of the one that had shown the way to win freedom, went the profound admiration of all. He was strengthened in the hope that India, as the friendly big brother, would guide those emergent nations and form with them a force for peace, a third force, holding the balance between East and West.

Not all nations at Bandung could be won over to non-alignment. There were also the representatives of Red China, and Nehru treated them with particular friendliness. Flowery phrases were exchanged about the lasting friendship between the two largest countries in the world. Flattering the Chinese became a habit with India's prime minister. Year after year, he had Krishna Menon sponsor China's admission to the United Nations. It became a regular show: the wily Indian delegate righteously pleading China's cause, and the United States rallying her friends to defeat his motion.

Though the Chinese army had smashed its way into the Tibetan highlands in 1950 and moved menacingly up to the Indian border along the Himalaya range, Nehru continued to speak of Indo-Chinese brotherhood. He was convinced the Chinese had too many problems back home to think of causing mischief in India. So, despite some grumbling among politicians of the opposition, he failed to shore up the country's defenses and continued to marshal all its strength for economic progress.

Nehru did not have to fear the few critical voices within the country. The masses were solidly behind him and gloried in the growing world-wide prestige he was accumulating, though India was a newcomer to the conference tables of the world and not a very strong one either. His countrymen applauded every step he took, even when, on occasions, it was inconsistent with his avowed philosophy.

In the fall of 1961 a military expedition was dispatched to take over Goa, a tiny Portuguese colony on the west coast and the last holdover of Western imperialism on Indian soil. There was little sympathy the world over for Portugal's stubborn, antiquated hanging-on to this possession, yet it was a curious spectacle to see the chief disciple of Gandhi order tiny Goa taken with guns and rockets. But in the streets of

Indian cities the populace went wild at the news of the "victory," and *Panditji's* stock soared to new heights.

Panditji was the unrivaled great man, the embodiment of the new India. "With the possible exception of the Pope," said an observer, "Nehru undoubtedly has the largest individual following of any man alive."

It is one of the strange contradictions of our century that India, so much under the shadow of a single strong personality, remained also one of the few true democracies in the world, almost the only one among the newly independent states. Nehru insisted that it be so after independence had been gained.

The Constituent Assembly provided for a federation of fifteen states and for a central government elected by popular vote. The venerable Dr. Prasad became India's first president, largely a ceremonial function, while to the prime minister fell the actual task of running the country. As in Great Britain, he and his cabinet are responsible to Parliament and must justify all their actions before this body.

In 1951–52 the first free elections were held, the largest in the world, involving over 173 million voters. Since then this astounding spectacle has been periodically repeated with a steadily growing electorate. Though the majority of votes were cast by illiterate peasants, it was for them a very serious business and was handled in an orderly fashion. The political scene was alive with controversy, and the freedom of the opposition was apparent to anybody who could read the newspapers. Nehru had put to shame the lame excuse of so many modern dictators that their people were "not ready for democracy."

A new code of law abolished polygamy and upgraded the general position of women. Against strong, and at times violent, pressure Nehru insisted on a complete separation of church and state. All religions received equal status.

Discrimination on account of caste was strictly forbidden. The new code actually favored the long-mistreated Untouchables, since it reserved for them 20 per cent of the legislative seats, 13 per cent of civil service posts and a certain number of places in the crowded schools and universities. One of the principal framers of the Indian constitution was the famous Untouchable leader B. R. Ambedkar.

Long before independence Nehru had been deeply committed to the fight against hunger and poverty. Mainly upon his urging, a reluctant Congress had begun long-range planning while still feuding with the British. Now the time had come to translate the blueprints into action.

Many feared the prime minister's frequently expressed leftist point of view. "He has so often called himself a socialist," they said. "Will he now throw the country into a radical uproar?"

They need not have worried. Nehru's socialism was no more radical than what had long been practiced in many Western countries, including Great Britain.

In 1951 a five-year plan of economic growth, the first in a series, was launched. The per capita income was to be raised from thirty-five to fifty-six dollars a *year*. At this rate it should take another twenty years for the average person's annual income to reach one hundred dollars, which points up how poor the average person is.

The government took over direct management of power and irrigation dams, mines, steel mills and other basic industries comprising the "public sector" of Indian economy. Most enterprises, however, were left within the "private sector," among them factories, shops, hotels, restaurants and stores of all sizes and descriptions. The private jute mills in Bengal hum with ceaseless activity, and there are giant industrial empires, such as the Tata Works, that compare with the American Ford or Kaiser enterprises.

Communist dictators have, again and again, made the mistake of neglecting the farmer's plow for the factory smokestack. But Nehru never forgot that India was basically a nation of peasants. Its strength had to come from the soil.

The First Five-Year Plan stressed agricultural improvement and a much-needed land reform. A network of cooperative centers, the so-called Village Community Schemes, was established. Under expert guidance the peasants learned about better seeds and modern care of livestock. Village wells were cleaned up, and child care was taught. Home industries, such as weaving, were introduced to provide cash income in between crops. Local leaders were trained to carry on after the experts had to move on. For thousands of villages this was the first contact with the twentieth century.

Land reform, the distribution of the large holdings among landless peasants, soon began to lag behind plans. The landholding class exerted strong political pressure and obstructed the reform program at every turn. Oddly enough, had Nehru been less democratic, it would have moved along faster. But, abhorring force, he insisted on persuasion. "I want to change the vested interests," he maintained. "I do not want to destroy them."

The prime minister did not shrink from using force against the Communist movement in his own country. Fully aware of the cruel suppression and the disregard of human dignity that is rampant under the sign of the hammer and sickle, he was determined to keep India free from the totalitarian menace. In 1957, when the Communists won a local election in the state of Kerala he insisted on ousting them from the state government. Though freedom of expression was very dear to him, he urged passage of the so-called Detention Act, mainly to curb the Communists at home, whom he called "a foul conspiracy based on fraud and deceit and violence to produce chaos in India." According to the U.S. State Department, there were "more Communists in jail in India than in any other country, with the possible exception of the Soviet Union."

No wonder that such behavior once earned him the title, "running dog of imperialism," from the Soviet newspaper *Pravda*.

Yet, though he had his knuckles rapped on occasion by the captive Communist press, Nehru continued on friendly diplomatic terms with both Soviet Russia and Red China. In fact, he underscored, whenever he could, old cultural ties between the two Asian giants, India and China, both of which had produced glorious civilizations and given the world great spiritual concepts. Both were now poor and technologically behind the times. Together they contained more than a third of the world's population.

The two countries were now engaged in a still-peaceful contest. Which system would prove superior in raising living standards, in bringing about progress and happiness? Would the ruthless authoritarian regime of China have the edge over India where things moved more slowly, but where men were free and had a voice in determining their own fate?

It was a breath-taking race, and the whole world was watching with fascination from a grandstand seat.

15.

10 TIN MURTI MARG

==================================

SPRING HAD COME EARLY in 1958. The Holi festival was here again, and gangs of noisy children roamed the streets and plazas of New Delhi. Their inevitable squirt guns wrought havoc with the clothing of every passer-by, but the victims only smiled or bought off their attackers with coins and sweets.

The children spied a lone figure in white, striding along under the stately trees, waving greetings to many grownups who bowed respectfully.

"Jawaharlal," shouted the boys, and the next moment a horde was upon him. They pelted him with fistfuls of colored powder which quickly dissolved under the thin jet-streams of water. In a matter of seconds his clothes were completely soaked. The colors had run together in a crazy pattern. From his forehead and cheeks dripped the messy liquid.

The prime minister thought this to be great fun and shook with hearty laughter. "Come on, boys," he shouted after he had caught his breath. "Come over to my garden. Let's have a party with my grandsons. They're waiting."

The invitation was met with shouts and cheers. They pressed around him and almost dragged him the few blocks toward his residence.

Several security guards hovered unhappily in the background. "This job is more frustrating than breaking rocks," murmured one. "Here we are, sworn to protect him. But how can we?"

"Impossible," answered his colleague. "And he always does that. Charges right into the thickest crowd where almost anybody can take a potshot at him. Toughest job to look after a man who is so popular."

In the spacious gardens that surrounded the Prime Minister's House, Rajiv and Sanjaya, Nehru's two grandsons, had taken command of the invasion forces. Feeling very important, they led the visitors along the neat walkways and around the ponds. Dogs barked furiously. Peacocks ruffled their beautiful long feathers and stalked off in disdain. The prime minister's two pet pandas took refuge behind some ornamental shrubs waiting for the furor to subside.

Grandpa Jawaharlal brought bags of sweetmeats and platters heaped with fruit. He seemed to have the time of his life as he dropped the gifts into the outstretched dirty hands.

He turned to an astonished foreign journalist waiting for a scheduled interview. "Children just take to me," explained the man whose own childhood had been a lonely one.

Ambassadors have cooled their heels in his anteroom while he was out attending a children's art show or chatting with patients in a children's hospital. Critics accused him of spending an inordinate amount of time and energy on such things as dedicating playgrounds or children's zoos. It became customary to celebrate his own birthday all over the country as Children's Day with youth rallies and carnivals. The prime minister had categorically forbidden it to be called Nehru Day, as he also ruled out the naming of streets or buildings after him. Otherwise the country would by now abound in Nehru Avenues, Nehru Plazas and Nehru Parks.

In many ways Jawaharlal Nehru was one of the most unusual specimens within the ranks of modern prime ministers.

His day began with yoga exercises, a habit acquired in prison. Yoga involves a slow stretching and flexing of the muscles very different from the jerky movements of Western calisthenics. Until his last illness a headstand was always included in his morning routine.

Whenever possible he had breakfast with his family, consisting now of his daughter Indira and her two sons. Then the boys took off for school, and Grandpa did not see them anymore till the next morning. But even this sort of family interlude was often interrupted by secretaries bringing dispatches to be read or documents to be signed. Important visitors sometimes shared the breakfast table, and then the conversation stuck to matters of state.

Indira was the official hostess for the widowed prime minister. She accompanied him on his travels and was probably the person in whom he confided more than in anybody else. Married to Feroze Gandhi, a member of Parliament, but no relation to the Mahatma, she had become a political figure in her own right. Her special interests were social welfare and cultural programs. In 1959 she was elected president of the Congress party, a post once held by her grandfather and later, many times, by her father. When she was, on occasion, mentioned as a possible successor to the prime ministry, there were subdued mutterings about a "Nehru dynasty."

After breakfast Jawaharlal would come downstairs to work. The Prime Minister's House at 10 Tin Murti Marg is an official residence like the White House. Calm and informality reign throughout the ornate Victorian building which was once the home of the British commander-in-chief. The only uniforms in evidence are those of the two *chaprassis,* the tall bearded doormen, clad in bright red, their eyes friendly and alert under the red turbans. If there are any other guards about, they are not distinguishable as such. There is none of the interminable checking and frisking often practiced in similar places.

Every morning the prime minister stepped out on the lawn where a sizable crowd awaited him. Townspeople and villagers came to meet him here in the morning hour. Straight from the heart they told him of their troubles, and he lis-

tened patiently to their complaints. Many just stood silently
and looked at their leader. Then they went away uplifted by
the *darshan,* a word which is hard to translate. It stands, ap-
proximately, for the blessing one receives from beholding a
great personality.

Only after the people had been comforted and reassured
by his presence, Nehru returned to his office, and the wheels
of state began to turn in earnest. Typists and secretaries
worked in shifts day and night. Instead of pushing buzzers
at his desk, the boss had the habit of personally popping into
various offices to see how things were going.

Nehru kept busy till late into the night and got along
with five hours of sleep. There was no change of pace on week
ends. His only relaxation now was an occasional turn through
the garden, where he kept track of shrubs that had begun to
bloom and where he liked to feed the animals, some in cages
and others running loose.

His health was superb till he reached his early seventies.
He could outwork associates many years his junior and out-
hike them on his rare vacations in the mountains. But then
he began to look tired and worn. Illness kept him away from
his desk for short periods.

Throughout his life Nehru was the object of controversy. Attacks upon him, both from inside and outside
the country, had been heated. He made many mistakes, and
unlike other powerful public figures, he candidly admitted
his errors or confessed that he did not always know the right
answers.

He obviously squandered too much time on nonessentials.
Before important conferences, he had been seen checking
the seating arrangements, like a head usher, and peeking
into inkwells to see if they were properly filled. To be sure
that things were done right, he would rather do them himself.
This reluctance to delegate responsibility actually made him
a poor administrator. When Nehru was away from his desk,
the machinery of government almost ground to a standstill.

His preoccupation with thoughts and ideas left him impatient with routine and details. Many were his masterful pronouncements of bold plans that were never put into effect. "He composes magnificent tunes," said one critic, "but bestows little care upon the orchestra."

A shrinking back from strong deeds, failure to take determined steps at a critical moment appeared to be Nehru's gravest shortcoming. Compromise rather than a sharply defined move suited his temper best, since he liked to look at events from the distant heights of the critical thinker. He always tried to see both sides of a controversy and could discover merit in different courses of action. Ruthlessness and fanaticism were completely alien to his mind. But delay and hesitancy could appear as weakness to friend and foe in the rough-and-ready game of practical politics.

Without a doubt, Nehru profoundly enjoyed the popular admiration that had so overwhelmingly been bestowed upon him. He would accept an unending flow of invitations to open scientific congresses or to celebrate anniversaries. Jokes circulated in the capital that there was no cornerstone in modern India that was not laid by Nehru.

Through his office moved an almost endless stream of foreign visitors: journalists, scholars, educators, who engaged him in conversations about the great issues confronting our times. Up to thirteen such interviews are known to have been scheduled in a single day. Nehru found these exchanges of wit and thought very stimulating, though they cut deeply into the time he needed to run his country.

In foreign politics, which he conducted almost singlehandedly, the hostility toward Pakistan remained a festering sore. Fifty per cent of India's meager armed forces were continuously tied up along the Pakistani borders, and the economic losses caused by the rift defy any measuring. Though a champion of the United Nations, Nehru steadfastly refused to let that international body settle the Kashmir issue.

"Any retreat in Kashmir," he reasoned, "may rekindle the bloody feud between Hindus and Moslems within our own republic."

His deliberate friendly gestures toward the Communist world continued to annoy the West. He exchanged cordial visits with the premier of Red China, who pledged "perpetual peaceful coexistence," and refused to be alarmed even after Peiping had begun to claim some 50,000 square miles of desolate Indian border territory adjoining Tibet and the province of Sinkiang. In repeated border raids the Chinese began to nibble away on this mountainous wasteland and even built a road through it but Nehru continued to believe that to show her lack of concern and her complete peacefulness was India's best protection. The towering, wind-swept borderlands remained unguarded, and the nation went undisturbed about its daily business.

This failure to read obvious handwriting on the wall may have had something to do with the fact that Nehru was not overly blessed with trusted advisers. Surrounded by worshipful crowds, he remained still a lonely figure. Nehru had never made friends easily. Particularly since the death of the Mahatma and the departure of the Mountbattens the circle of intimates had shrunk drastically. There were, of course, ever-devoted Indira and Krishna Menon. Recalled from his post at the United Nations, Krishna Menon was made Minister of Defense. From his bachelor's quarters right opposite the Prime Minister's House he slipped almost daily across the street for intimate consultation.

Not well known to the general public was M. O. Mathai, Nehru's special assistant, who lived in his official home and was constantly by his side. Through his close contacts with the prime minister, his influence might have been considerable.

Nehru managed not always to behave according to the diplomatic code of etiquette. Impatient with fools and with pompous mediocrity, he had been seen yawning at official receptions or looking out the window with extreme boredom on his face during long-winded speeches. Meaningless protocol annoyed him greatly. With a chuckle he recalled how one of his ambassadors threatened to go home because, at an official dinner, "he was seated to the left of somebody instead of to the right."

A growing concern to friends of India everywhere was the fact that Nehru failed to attract and train a group of younger leaders. "After Nehru what?" became a question asked with rising urgency. Jawaharlal himself, however, did not seem to be bothered by it, despite his advanced age. "There are many bright and capable people in India," he contended, "and I trust the democratic process to bring them to the fore when the need arises."

All this added up to quite a lengthy list of weaknesses, but they still were the weaknesses of a great man. He would not have been Jawaharal Nehru, the courageous, selfless humanist, the product of two cultures, the compromiser of divergent ideals, had he not possessed all sorts of shortcomings that resulted from his unique position and mental make-up. Whatever the flaws, his position in history has been assured for several decades.

The greatest accomplishment of India is that she has survived, and it is doubtful if this could have happened without Nehru. India was no nation before independence; she had to be made into one. To weld the odd conglomeration of religions, castes and language groups into one community was a task of superhuman proportions. It took a giant to force unrelenting progress in all these fields on a reluctant population.

Caste prejudice, though outlawed, still persists, especially in the backward rural areas. But the pace of social change is quickening, and a new wind is blowing even to the remotest villages.

The language problem is charged with explosive danger. Passions have repeatedly been aroused to a fever pitch over the question of what should be the official language in a particular state of the republic. There are at least fourteen major languages, in addition to several hundred dialects that have never been written down.

During Mogul days, Persian was the court language, and the members of the Nehru family were very familiar with it. It was superseded by English, still the only tongue in which people from various parts of the republic can communicate. The business of the central government is largely carried on in English.

Only a tiny segment, namely the educated groups, speak English. This tends to widen the gap between the upper class and the masses. The nationalistic spirit also balks at the use of a language brought to India by its former oppressors.

Official plans call for a native language, Hindi, to eventually replace English in the courts and government offices, as well as at the universities. Many people ask, "Why *Hindi?* Why not the language used in our part of the country?" In the face of bitter agitation and even violence, Nehru, himself a master of the English language, brought about a characteristic compromise: regional languages in the various states, but a gradual introduction of Hindi as the official all-India language. English should be used as long as necessary and should continue as the favorite foreign language for study in the schools.

Nehru, at times, appeared slow in taking decisive action, but he never wavered on matters of principle. The idea of a nonsectarian government and the equality of all religions were fundamental convictions which he would uphold against even the most dangerous pressure. Two Moslems served in his cabinet and several were on his personal staff. They filled important positions in the civil service and in the armed forces. India's Moslems looked to the prime minister as their chief protector.

In 1961 he successfully repulsed the fiery demands of the Sikh community for a separate state within the republic. "No state boundaries along religious lines," he declared and he remained steadfast even when the revered Sikh leader,

Master Tara Singh, employed a weapon from Gandhi's arsenal. He went on a fast "to death," but when Nehru refused to be intimidated, he gave up after several days.

Widespread ignorance and illiteracy, especially in the villages, remained high on Jawaharlal's list of evils to be fought. Knowing well the peasant's hunger for knowledge, he drove the educational planners to ever-greater haste. By 1962 twenty million children were crowding the very primitive schoolrooms. The number is growing continuously, but it will still take years till every child will have a school to go to.

Though lacking interest and training in practical economics, Nehru remained the unchallenged mastermind of long-range economic planning. Progress is slow, and much of it is offset by the rapidly increasing population. By 1970 it will amount to five hundred million. Better health care and improved sanitation now stretch the average life span to forty-two years and create a population explosion.

The Western visitor still shudders as he beholds the abysmal poverty clinging to Indian cities. In Calcutta hundreds of thousands of human beings sleep on the sidewalks every night. College graduates find no jobs suited to their newly acquired skills. They become frustrated and restless, the ideal victims of Communist propaganda.

Yet, there are now more rich people in India than ever before, and—what is particularly significant—there is a rapidly growing middle class of business and professional men, of white-collar workers and public officials, who live in modern apartments and are beginning to enjoy many of the amenities that have become commonplace to us.

Economic advances are evident everywhere, on the broad urban avenues and also along the narrow dusty highways where incredibly crowded buses and rattling trucks and jeeps tread their way carefully through slow-moving flocks of sheep. From the age of padding bare feet, said Nehru, "we have not yet advanced to the age of the automobile, but we have arrived at the age of the bicycle."

With advancing years, Jawaharlal appeared to become less impatient. Wherever possible, he wanted to depend on self-help, rather than on foreign help. "It is better to go a little slower and rely on yourself than to become dependent." Nevertheless, tokens of economic aid came from Russia and other Communist countries, whereas from the West, particularly from the United States, a steady stream of assistance had poured in, despite differences in political viewpoints as his life drew to a close. Nehru had come to understand America better, especially after cordial meetings with two of our presidents, Dwight Eisenhower and John Kennedy. Several American ambassadors and other statesmen became his good friends, and Mrs. Jacqueline Kennedy seemed to have charmed him completely on her visit to India.

In the conference rooms of world politics he continued to be a voice of sanity. War remained for him the all-consuming evil. Every rattling of weapons, especially of thermonuclear weapons, may bring the absurdity of war closer and should be banned from the face of the earth. "With the coming of nuclear weapons," he declared, "war seems to us—and seems to most people everywhere—an extreme folly, that is, it has ceased to promise what you want."

In the great awakening of Asia and Africa Nehru towered as the outstanding spokesman of the middle way between hostile extremes, the statesman-philosopher whose mind remained open to diverse streams of thought, who denied all highhanded claims to absolute truth. A warm upsurge of pride filled the hearts of Indians seeing the respect that Nehru had generated on the international stage.

Through the new nation's painful ascent from suppression and backwardness, through all the complications and setbacks, he was the guide, scolding the laggard, encouraging the weary, teaching the ignorant. India's politicians knew that, while Nehru did not need them, they needed Nehru. Lacking in political experience, the members of Parliament willingly submitted to his leadership so that Nehru appeared to some students of politics as a dictator despite himself.

He remained the undisputed leader of the Congress party whether or not he carried the title of its president at the moment, but the ruling political party lost much of its old revolutionary fervor. Lust for spoils and patronage replaced the sacrificial zeal of Gandhian days. Nobody lashed out more bitterly against Congress corruption and complacency than Nehru, but his verbal chastisements could rouse Congress only temporarily. Then the powerful political machine sank back into petty bickering and the enjoyment of the rich spoils.

Nehru felt like a man trying to swim up a muddy river and making no headway despite the most grueling exertion.

The spring days were still pleasant and cool in New Delhi, but a foreboding of the long crushing summer was already in the air. The streets had been cleaned from the leavings of the Holi revelers.

Parliament struggled through a host of involved issues. The members had adjourned for the day, but they were reluctant to leave. During the proceedings a rumor had swept from bench to bench. Many faces showed agitation. A messenger hurried about, "Important caucus meeting of the Congress party in the courtyard. Please come right away."

The yard was crowded. Reporters and photographers mingled with the politicians. Something important was about to break.

The chairman of the parliamentary delegation raised his arm. "Your attention, friends. The prime minister wants to speak."

Nehru stood on the steps leading to the assembly hall. Many a Congress worker noticed how he had aged lately. His face looked gray. Even the rose in his buttonhole had wilted, and its petals drooped sadly. As he took off the white cap to wipe the perspiration from his forehead, the fringe of white hair appeared thin around the shining baldness of his skull.

"Give me your attention. I am tired and I want to go home. So I'm only going to keep you a minute."

They fell silent. Everybody pressed forward. A tight mass surrounded him.

"Things have come to a point where I must call a halt. Many of you don't seem to understand where I am heading, and I, somehow, cannot make you see things my way. I am losing my grip. Enough of all the arguing. At times I am not sure myself what I want. I feel stale and flat. I need to get away for a while to think, to read, to gain some perspective. Therefore I have decided to resign. Let somebody else—"

Individual shouts of dismay had interrupted his words and punctuated each sentence. Now the shouting had become general. It drowned out the voice of the old man. He stood, a picture of loneliness and dejection.

"No—no—no!" they cried.

"India needs you."

"The party cannot do without you."

"Where is your loyalty to Gandhi's party?"

"Don't leave us now."

The chairman flailed his arms through the air and tried to outshout the general babble. Finally a semblance of order was restored. The undisciplined outcries were replaced by a series of speeches, passionate, pleading, begging, even threatening. Many in the crowd sincerely feared that, without Nehru at the helm, India might sink back into chaos, and the gains, so painfully made, might be lost forever. Others were mainly worried about their own positions and offices. They saw the leading role of the Congress party threatened once it lost its universally revered leader.

The few minutes for which the prime minister had asked stretched into one solid hour, then into two.

At their residence Indira was waiting for the return of her father. With her were a few hungry dinner guests. Finally the car with the prime minister's pennant on the hood turned into the gently curved driveway. As Nehru stepped out, a siege of weakness seemed to overcome him, and he had to support himself by holding on to the door of the vehicle.

"I gave in," he replied to the wordless question on her face. "I am still the prime minister."

As he uttered the words, a change came over him. Drawing on some hidden reserves of strength, he let go of the door and stood erect. With firm steps he walked into his official residence.

16.

I HAVE ALSO SEEN

JAWAHARLAL NEHRU carried on.

To make him withdraw his resignation, party delegates and regional leaders had promised to support all his bills in Parliament and to stop all graft and jockeying for personal power. For a few weeks a new spirit seemed to pervade the old Congress machine, but then the intriguing and bickering began all over again.

The courtyard scene in the spring of 1958 repeated itself several times in somewhat different forms and in different places, but always with the same result. More and more Nehru himself came to believe that only he could bring off the gigantic task of India's rejuvenation.

The work continued at a man-killing pace. Step two of the great economic pull from the bullock age to the machine age was now in full swing. The Second Five-Year Plan had begun in 1956; the Third was to get off the ground in 1961. At its conclusion India was to produce enough food for all her people. Steel mills built by Britain, Russia and the United States were to be in full production. Indian factories were to turn out machine tools in quantity with which to set in motion vast industrial activity all over the country.

Peace was needed more than ever to keep the grandiose plans moving on schedule. But from their newly conquered strongholds in Tibet, Red Chinese patrols began to probe more brazenly into Indian territory. Chinese laborers even built a strategic road from Tibet to the province of Sinkiang leading through Indian territory. When newspapers and opposition leaders showed alarm, Nehru shrugged those events off as unimportant and called the seized areas "barren mountaintops where not a blade of grass grows."

Being a historian of note himself, he should have learned a lesson from the past: appeasement only encourages the aggressor and whets his appetite for bigger bites.

In the election campaign of 1962 the various parties competed for the votes of 125 million eligible Indians. Many had to vote by dropping marbles of different colors into the ballot boxes or by marking ballots on which the various parties were represented by the heads of bullocks, monkeys and other animals.

The most heated campaigning was done in the district of North Bombay where Krishna Menon was running for reelection to Parliament. Only as a duly elected member of Parliament could he continue to hold the office of Minister of Defense. Posters of opposition parties showed two red bayonets stabbing from China into India, and the caption read, "Menon represents China, not India." The wrath about the continued humiliations inflicted by the Chinese turned against the cocky chief adviser of the prime minister.

It was one of Nehru's weaknesses that loyalty to friends blinded him to their faults. He threw himself into the campaign with full vigor. He put all his popularity on the table. Against the stiffest opposition yet encountered during his regime, against a lukewarm attitude even in his own party, he pulled Krishna Menon through to a close victory.

Eight months later a long dream was shattered by a cruel awakening. On the twentieth of October, 1962, Communist China invaded the land of their "Asian brothers" in force. The rat-tat-tat of machine guns, the boom of mountain artillery, the burps of bazookas, suddenly pierced the eternal howling of the storms on Karakoram Pass and in the dents of the Himalaya Range on the frontier of Assam State. Before the unexpected onslaught bewildered Indian border guards fell back in confusion, outnumbered four to one and more. Hastily summoned reserves were soundly defeated on icy battlefields, 14,000 feet high. Accustomed to a steamy jungle climate, they were no match for hundreds of thousands of Chinese veterans who had been exposed to rigorous mountain training.

India rose with a roar like a bear suddenly disturbed in his hibernation. City streets resounded with the shouts of furious masses. Anger and wounded pride had replaced lethargy.

The garden of the prime minister's residence, still soaked in the early morning dew, was densely filled, and the crowd spilled over into driveways and streets. They had come not only for *darshan,* but also to express their readiness to make sacrifices.

"Five *rupees*—one *rupee*—ten *annas*—three *rupees.* Next, please."

The man at the table sang out the figures in a monotonous voice and made entries in a greasy, dog-eared ledger. People, waiting in a long line, stepped up to him, one by one. They were mostly women, shivering in the coolness of the November morning, but there was also a sprinkling of little schoolboys and of toothless graybeards.

An open tent had been erected, a makeshift branch of the national bank, to receive the gifts that were piling up on the oblong tables. There were not only heaps of coins and stacks of paper money, but also rings, gold pins and masses of bangles, the kind that jingle from almost every woman's wrist or ankle.

Morning after morning, since the beginning of the invasion, this scene had repeated itself. An endless flood of mail added to the contributions of rich and poor for the defense of the threatened country.

Now all eyes turned. Nehru appeared on the porch, dressed in his familiar tight white trousers, frock coat and white cap, with a fresh rose in the third buttonhole. For a moment he

surveyed the scene from the steps, his hands raised in the
namaste greeting. Then he turned to the waiting automobile.

Whispering followed the sudden silence of the crowd.

"How pale he looks and how tired."

"He probably hasn't slept all night."

"What grief for him. Those dirty Chinese dogs."

In silence Nehru rode the short distance to Parliament.
Along the way he saw men digging shallow trenches, a pitiful
attempt at air-raid defense. Students were lined up before a
recruiting station. On a park lawn a group of young women
were being drilled in precision marching by a burly Sikh
army sergeant.

Parliament was seething with discontent. The prime minister sat on the government bench, shoulders hunched under
the invisible weight of historical miscalculation. Angry
speeches were interrupted by even angrier shouts from the
floor.

"Why weren't we prepared?"

"What was the defense minister doing the last five years?"

"Was the defense minister working for Communist China
or for India?"

"Krishna Menon must go."

"Krishna Menon—Krishna Menon—" The unpopular
name was shouted from a hundred angry lips. Whatever the
defense minister's share of guilt, he was now the universal
scapegoat. But his old protector knew that the cries for
Krishna Menon's scalp were also an unspoken reproach
against himself. For the first time in fifteen years, he felt
himself dragged along by his party and his parliament instead of leading them.

Nehru rose to speak. With that honesty he had displayed
all his public life, he refused to hide behind lame excuses
and gloss over unpleasant facts. He described the humiliating
military defeat in all its hapless details. Carrying grotesquely
outmoded single-shot rifles, the defenders had simply been
wiped off the mountains by the murderous fire of Chinese

automatic weapons. At least 2,500 Indians had been killed in the first few days, and over 6,000 were missing. Not only all the disputed areas, but many thousand additional square miles of truly Indian territory had been overrun.

What explanation could he give?

"Our thinking was naïve. India is a democracy unconditioned for conflict, whereas Communist China has prepared for war. It was naked large-scale aggression—premeditated and concerted and obviously undertaken after long preparation and deliberate planning—"

A low growl of dissatisfaction rose from the benches. These were not the words they wanted to hear.

"We are all guilty," continued the chief executive.

The murmur grew louder. Enough of the breast-beating. They wanted action, not pious statements about India's innocence. Even the faces of the Congress delegates were sullen. Their usual docility was gone. They were in no mood to just listen and applaud.

For a moment the seventy-three year-old prime minister stood motionless. His face was a mask behind which hid contempt for the fickleness of his followers and also grief over his own lack of foresight.

He took a deep breath. His back straightened. The murmuring ceased. The electric tension preceding an important moment was in the air. Nehru's voice was low, barely audible:

"For the best interest of the nation, the Honorable Krishna Menon has submitted his resignation from his cabinet post. I have accepted it with deep regret because—"

They cheered. They were not interested in the eulogy. Nobody wanted to hear Nehru praise his old friend who finally had to be sacrificed to almost universal criticism. Now everybody was satisfied. No word of blame against the former defense minister's boss was uttered. The scapegoat had been driven out into the wilderness loaded with everybody's sins.

He continued:

"The first planeload of desperately needed arms from the United States of America has arrived—" The house rose in jubilation as if a victory had just been proclaimed.

"American planes carrying infantry weapons and ammunition are landing at the rate of one every three hours. Great Britain and our friends of the Commonwealth are also preparing to send aid."

Then, remembering his long-standing role as the apostle of nonalignment, he hastily added, "The good wishes of the Soviet Union are a great consolation to us, and we hope we will have them in the future. We must realize we cannot suggest that they go against their allies—"

This was the balance sheet of neutrality in the cold war: five million dollars' worth of weapons from the United States, practically within hours, and further unlimited help pledged, as against the "good wishes" of the Soviets, plus the vague hope that they would honor a long-standing promise of a dozen MIG jets sometime in the dim future. It was not easy for the man in the driver's seat to unlearn some faulty lessons of the past.

The Parliament session ended with a rousing vote of confidence for Nehru. Then he was off to address a mass rally. From a rickety wooden platform braced by stout bamboo staves he spoke to over fifty thousand countrymen: society women, shopkeepers, peasants. Squatting side by side on the hard ground they were hanging on every movement of his lips. Once again Jawaharlal was taking his cause to the masses, and the old magic still proved effective. Under the spell of his words, a nation, aflame with indignation, became, at long last, united in the face of threatening catastrophe. As if by the waving of a sorcerer's wand, the language and caste barriers had become invisible. Indistinguishable from each other, an ocean of white garments crowned by bobbing brown faces, they sat entranced and listened.

"—We will never rest till the enemy is expelled from our soil. But it will mean heavy sacrifices. The war may last for years. We must forget any grudge of Indian against Indian and all work together. China has done us a favor by waking up the whole country—"

They went away heartened and hopeful that as long as *Panditji* was guiding them, everything would come out all right in the end.

Panditji returned to his office, his mind a battlefield of contradictory thoughts. So now he was a war leader, a strange role for the man who had so long been scolding the statesmen of the world for their violent words and militant gestures. Would Gandhiji have approved? Of course, he would, for he hated cowardice even more than he hated violence.

But Nehru was no Gandhi. He did not have the Mahatma's unshakable self-assurance, the certainty that he was moving in the right direction. Nor was he another Churchill, who could sound convincing in the role of the lusty warrior. He was just a misplaced man of good will, disciple of Eastern prophets and Western humanists, ill-suited for the blood-and-thunder pep talks soldiers about to face the enemy wanted to hear.

Yet it was Nehru, and only Nehru, who, if anybody, could rally this ill-prepared, ill-equipped nation into battle formation. Had he insisted on resigning his post, he would have spared himself the present mental anguish. The future was uncertain, and it demanded a drastic re-evaluation of convictions held for many years.

"India will never be the same again." These were the words of B. K. Nehru, Indian ambassador to the United States and a relative of the prime minister's. Nor could Jawaharlal himself ever be quite the same, though he insisted that his basic policy was still valid.

He had humbled himself by pleading with the Western powers for help. They had responded speedily and generously not only to keep the Communist avalanche from rolling closer to their own borders, but also to keep the great

Indian experiment of progress by democratic means from failing.

On the other hand, Russia, apprehensive of China's growing influence in Asia, advised that he stop fighting and accept Peking's border claims. And all this while Chinese soldiers were still shooting their way deeper into Indian territory.

One by one, noncommitted neighbors, once loud in supporting Nehru's stand, begged off from making common cause with the attacked nation. They used many words masking their lack of appetite to do anything that might bring the wrath of China upon them.

The whole political picture was out of focus. The Western "imperialist" governments were the only ones coming to the former colony's help as it was attacked by fellow Asians. The West was also urging upon Nehru a new look at the vexing Kashmir issue that still poisoned relations with Pakistan. Eight badly needed Indian divisions were tied up along the Pakistan border. As long as the teeming peninsula was rent by inner conflict, defense against outside invasion seemed almost hopeless.

What did it all mean? Why had China undertaken this surprise campaign? She certainly had enough land and people of her own. There was no crying need for some more barren rock in an ill-defined twilight region that counted among the most inhospitable places in the world.

The Red bosses had been plagued by severe economic reverses at home. Did they hope the military victories would divert the minds of their grumbling subjects from their own dismal lives? Were they alarmed over the progress democratic India was making? Was all this to discredit India and to make her lose face in the eyes of the Afro-Asian world whose leader she wanted to be?

Where did the rift between Moscow and Peking fit in, the quarrel over who possessed the true Communist doctrine? And what about the concept of nonalignment? Had it completely lost its meaning?

All these questions confronted an uneasy world as it watched the storm clouds gather in the Himalaya Mountains and then saw the storm break out in hurricane strength on October 20, 1962.

A pall of anxiety hung over many capitals. In this period of interlocking pacts and intertwined national interests, any conflict, remote as it might seem, could be the torch that would light a universal conflagration. But suddenly, at the height of her victories, China stopped the attacks and proclaimed a unilateral cease-fire. As mysteriously as it had begun, the shooting sputtered to a halt and an uneasy calm settled over the icy mountain passes. But the Red armies remained poised for fresh strikes at a moment of their own choosing.

Why had China put the brakes on her war machine just when the going was good? It is hard to follow the twists and turns in the policies of a government that operates in secrecy and need not render account to its people. The Communist leaders may have become aware of the overwhelming difficulties in supplying their armies over lengthening communication lines in the dead of winter. They may have been startled by the West's apparent determination to stand by India. A full-scale confrontation with the industrial might of the United States and her allies was not what Peking had bargained for.

Besides, one goal had already been achieved: the chief Asian rival was humiliated. India's lack of military prowess had been demonstrated before the world, and her neighbors were shaking with fear of the Chinese colossus.

While the Indian republic was reeling under the physical blows delivered to her armies and under the mental shock of seeing her whole destiny threatened, the life of Jawaharlal Nehru was slowly ebbing away. In January 1964 he suffered a paralytic stroke on his way to a party meeting. The often dreaded vacuum in top government was now a reality, for

Nehru had stubbornly refused to designate or groom a successor.

Subordinates kept the governmental wheels turning as best they could. The top administrative decisions were now in the hands of Lal Bahadur Shastri, Minister Without Portfolio, a slight colorless man of modest background and strong Gandhian roots. Luckily Y. B. Chavan who had succeeded Krishna Menon as defense minister deported himself with vigor and determination which was just what the nation needed.

With more urgency than ever before, India asked the question, "After Nehru what?" No clear answer was forthcoming. For a short interval the questioning was muted to a whisper by the Pandit's return from the sickbed. Against medical advice he resumed his gruelling schedule, a man in a hurry who knew how little time was left. Seeing his whole life's work in jeopardy, he tried to squeeze an unbelievable amount of activities into his waking hours. But it was no use. To everybody, if not to himself, it was obvious that the man who still insisted on giving interviews and making speeches was only a shadow of the old freedom fighter.

His skin was flabby and his back stooped. Weakened by the stroke, his left foot dragged behind the right one. In Parliament he sat deeply hunched struggling to keep awake, and when he rose to answer questions, his speech was halting, and he had to grip the edge of his desk to keep erect. Once when he tried to defend his Congress Party against new accusations of flagrant corruption, there were cries of "resign, resign" from the benches of the younger deputies. Those were sounds never heard before during the long Nehru era.

The debacle on the Himalaya frontier had tarnished his prestige in the foreign ministries of the world. Once his words were received with deep respect despite the poverty of his country. Now they were shrugged off as coming from a man whose judgment had been found grievously faulty.

Only for the faceless mass, the four hundred-odd million average Indians in town and village, *Panditji* remained to the end the beloved father-figure, the heir to the Mahatma, who had pointed the way toward a brighter future and had sacrificed so much in its behalf. At one of his last outings, when he was riding through the streets of Calcutta, the crowds, as usual, pierced the thin police lines. The car was halted by a solid wall of worshipful admirers. Above all the noise could be heard the shrill shout of a boy clinging to the top of a telephone pole. Quavering with excitement, as if he had just beheld a heavenly apparition, he repeated, "I have also seen. I have also seen."

To the end Nehru's mind was a battlefield between two contradictory traits: a strong emotional commitment that demanded action and a desire to compromise. In the long argument over Kashmir he had shown himself unrelenting, and the danger-charged issue remained a sorry piece of unfinished business. Though the specter of Chinese aggression continued to hover over the northern valleys, India's finest combat troops were still facing the armies of Pakistan which voiced increased resentment over Western military aid to the Nehru government.

Prodded by the democratic countries, the two neighbors made a new effort to straighten out their difficulties. There was a flurry of negotiations, but they soon bogged down in the mire of old distrust and jealousy.

Then, only eight weeks before his death, the Prime Minister startled the subcontinent with a dramatic gesture. He ordered the release of Sheik Mohammed Abdullah, the Kashmiri Moslem leader, who had been imprisoned for ten years for protesting India's rule over his home state. The two had once been comrades in the independence movement, but then their ways had parted. Sheik Mohammed stood for self-determination of Kashmir where the strong Moslem majority would probably, in the end, have hoped to join Pakistan. Jawaharlal steadfastly refused to let the mountain state slip from India's grasp, and not only because he was personally so deeply attached to the home of his ancestors. He also feared that the agitation over a plebiscite, as demanded by Pakistan, and any further loss of Kashmiri territory might touch off renewed bloodshed between Hindus and Moslems all over the scarred face of India. Now Sheik Mohammed came from his cell to confer with the Prime Minister and then took off on a mysterious visit to the Pakistani capital.

But it was too late for a drastic surgical graft that would close the wound. Nehru had just returned from a six-day visit to Dehra-Dun in the Himalayas, the hunting grounds of his youth, where he had hoped to find relief and rejuvenation. On the morning of May 27, 1964 he awoke with severe pains in his shoulders. The seventy-four-year-old premier lapsed into a coma. Eight hours later, C. Subramaniam, a member of the cabinet, stood before Parliament and repeated the words Nehru himself had once uttered at the death of his *guru*, "The light has gone out."

From the benches crowded with hardened politicians rose the sound of weeping. The chief minister's seat, occupied by the same man for seventeen years, was empty.

In the midst of the unfinished play the master actor had been taken from the stage. He had missed the moment when he could have made his exit in glory, his image untarnished by personal failure. Why did he stay on? The answer is as complicated as was Jawaharlal's character. Certainly his vanity, which he shared with so many other public figures, forbade him to acknowledge that others could do the job as well. But there was more to it. Friend and foe admitted freely that his personality, almost alone, had kept the loose fabric that was modern India from disintegrating. When doubt and despair would have been more justified, he had instilled in his countrymen a sense of identity and purpose. He was aware of it and he felt duty-bound not to desert his post.

The many contradictions which battled in his mind had made him deeply and charmingly human. He was born to wealth, but in sympathy with socialism, aristocratically aloof and yet an idol of the masses. A man of action in love with the machine age, he yearned to read, write and meditate in solitude. An internationalist who was thoroughly at ease with the ways of the West, he has his place in history as the standard-bearer of Indian nationalism.

Even in death Jawaharlal Nehru remained a study in ironic contradiction. The life-long agnostic and modernist was committed to eternity under strictest observance of ancient religious ritual which he would have found outdated and superstitious. Under a scorching sun three million mourners lined the route of the funeral procession softly chanting sacred verses. Four persons were crushed to death.

On the Rajghat by the holy Jammu River, only three hundred yards from Gandhi's cremation spot, the Prime Minister's body was placed on a pyre of sandalwood cushioned with roses and marigold. Two saffron-robed priests conducted Sandjay Gandhi, Indira's seventeen-year-old son, to the body. The youth folded his grandfather's hands on the chest, anointed him with holy water and then touched a burning torch to the sandalwood.

As the first flames began to lick at the white shroud, the priests chanted, "He is free of earthly bondage."

Showering flower petals on the burning pyre, the crowd responded, "May he be immortal."

BIBLIOGRAPHY

Bowles, Chester. *Ambassador's Report*. Harper & Bros., New York, 1954.

Brecher, Michael. *Nehru: A Political Biography*. Oxford University Press, London, 1959.

Cousins, Norman. *Talks with Nehru*. John Day, New York, 1951.

Edwardes, Michael. *Nehru, A Pictorial Biography*. Viking Press, New York, 1962.

Fischer, Louis. *The Life of Mahatma Gandhi*. Collier, New York, 1950.

Hutheesing, Krishna (Nehru). *With No Regrets*. John Day, New York, 1945.

Mende, Tibor. *Nehru: Conversations on India and World Affairs*. Braziller, New York, 1956.

Menon, K. N. *Children's Nehru*. Caxton Press, New Delhi, 1960.

Moraes, Frank. *India Today*. Macmillan, New York, 1960.

————. *Jawaharlal Nehru. A Biography*. Macmillan, New York, 1956.

Nanda, B. R. *The Nehrus, Motilal and Jawaharlal*. John Day, New York, 1962.

Nehru, Jawaharlal. *The Discovery of India*. John Day, New York, 1945.

————. *Glimpses of World History*. John Day, New York, 1942.

————. *Independence and After. A Collection of Speeches 1946–1949*. John Day, New York, 1950.

————. *Toward Freedom. The Autobiography of Jawaharlal Nehru*. John Day, New York, 1941.

————. *The Unity of India*. John Day, New York, 1942.

————. *Visit to America*. John Day, New York, 1950.

Palmer, Norman D. *The Indian Political System*. Houghton Mifflin, Boston, 1961.

Sheean, Vincent. *Nehru: The Years of Power*. Random House, New York, 1960.

Sing, Anup. *Nehru: The Rising Star of India*. John Day, New York, 1939.

Spear, Percival. *India: A Modern History*. University of Michigan Press, Ann Arbor, 1961.

INDEX

187

About the Author

ALFRED APSLER was born in Vienna, Austria, in 1907 and is now an American citizen. He began writing in his student years, and has been a contributor to newspapers and magazines in Europe and the United States and author of trade books and textbooks. Since 1943 he has taught in high schools and colleges in Oregon and Washington. At present he is Chairman of the Social Science Division of Clark College in Vancouver, Washington, where he lives with his wife and two children.